MW01071614

Praise For

Joy Prescriptions

"Emotional health is a crucial ingredient to overall well-being. *Joy Prescriptions* connects the two components of living well, offering actionable insights on living with intention, balance, and vibrancy."

—**Casey Means, MD,** #1 *New York Times* best-selling author of *Good Energy*

"As the first Chinese American Real Housewife, Tiffany is no stranger to breaking free from cultural expectations while staying true to her roots. *Joy Prescriptions* is a beautifully authentic reflection for anyone navigating the complexities of identity and fulfillment."

—**Crystal Kung Minkoff,** cofounder of Real Coco and star of Bravo's *The Real Housewives of Beverly Hills*

"Reading *Joy Prescriptions* feels like sitting down with a wise friend. Tiffany tackles the pressure to be perfect, the guilt of wanting more, and the fear of letting others down, some of the most pressing issues of self-worth facing women today. I love the 'joy prescriptions' she provides at the end of each chapter."

—**Nicole Martin, MD,** board-certified anesthesiologist and star of Bravo's *The Real Housewives of Miami*

"*Joy Prescriptions* is a testament to the power of resilience. With vulnerability and wisdom, she reminds us that joy isn't something we stumble upon—it's something we cultivate through gratitude, connection, and self-compassion."

—**Amanda Ngoc Nguyen,** astronaut, social activist, and Nobel Peace Prize nominee

"As someone who works in a field where perfection is often highly valued, I am constantly seeking ways to embrace spontaneity and connection. *Joy Prescriptions* is a powerful reminder to focus on what truly matters, and it is a book that everyone, no matter their stage in life, can learn from."

—**Anthony Youn, MD,** board-certified plastic surgeon and author of national bestseller *Younger for Life*

"Embracing imperfection is what brings depth, character, and richness to our lives. The era of masking struggles with a forced smile to climb the ladder is behind us. This book offers the exact guide I wish I had to navigate life's demands while prioritizing genuine joy and meaningful purpose."

—**Betsy Grunch, MD,** board-certified neurosurgeon

JOY
PRESCRIPTIONS

How I Learned to
Stop Chasing Perfection
and Embrace Connection

TIFFANY MOON, MD

LEGACY
LIT

New York Boston

Copyright © 2025 by Tiffany Moon
Cover design by Amanda Kain
Cover photograph by Jonny Ngo
Cover copyright © 2025 by Hachette Book Group, Inc.

Hachette Book Group supports the right to free expression and the value of copyright. The purpose of copyright is to encourage writers and artists to produce the creative works that enrich our culture.

The scanning, uploading, and distribution of this book without permission is a theft of the author's intellectual property. If you would like permission to use material from the book (other than for review purposes), please contact Permissions@hbgusa.com. Thank you for your support of the author's rights.

Legacy Lit
Hachette Book Group
1290 Avenue of the Americas
New York, NY 10104
LegacyLitBooks.com
@LegacyLitBooks

First Edition: April 2025

Legacy Lit is an imprint of Grand Central Publishing. The Legacy Lit name and logo are registered trademarks of Hachette Book Group, Inc.

The publisher is not responsible for websites (or their content) that are not owned by the publisher.

The Hachette Speakers Bureau provides a wide range of authors for speaking events. To find out more, visit hachettespeakersbureau.com or email HachetteSpeakers@hbgusa.com.

Legacy Lit books may be purchased in bulk for business, educational, or promotional use. For information, please contact your local bookseller or email the Hachette Book Group Special Markets Department at Special.Markets@hbgusa.com.

Print book interior design by Amy Quinn

Library of Congress Cataloging-in-Publication Data

Name: Moon, Tiffany, author.
Title: Joy prescriptions: how I overcame perfectionism to embrace gratitude, love, and laughter / Tiffany Moon.
Description: First edition. | New York, NY: Legacy Lit, [2025]
Identifiers: LCCN 2024036577 | ISBN 9780306834530 (hardcover) | ISBN 9780306834547 (trade paperback) | ISBN 9780306834554 (ebook)
Subjects: LCSH: Self-acceptance. | Perfectionism (Personality trait) | Self-realization. | Conduct of life.
Classification: LCC BF575.S37 M66 2025 | DDC 158.1—dc23/eng/20250206
LC record available at https://lccn.loc.gov/2024036577

ISBNs: 978-0-306-83453-0 (hardcover); 978-0-306-83455-4 (ebook)

Printed in the United States of America

LSC-C

Printing 1, 2025

For my girls—may your lives be filled with so much joy

CONTENTS

Introduction   *How I Learned to Stop Chasing Perfection
and Embrace Connection*   ix

Part I

CHAPTER 1   **CHOOSE YOUR OWN ADVENTURE**   3
            Joy Prescription: Let Go of the Past

CHAPTER 2   **COMPARE AND CONTRAST**   21
            *Joy Prescription: Break Free from
            Comparison*

CHAPTER 3   **BLINDERS**   35
            *Joy Prescription: Focus on the Journey,
            Not the Destination*

CHAPTER 4   **GOOD ON PAPER**   55
            *Joy Prescription: Be Open to Love in
            Unexpected Places*

Part II

CHAPTER 5   **UNCHARTED TERRITORY**   75
            *Joy Prescription: Accept What You Can't
            Control and Focus on What You Can*

CHAPTER 6   **YES-WOMAN**   93
            *Joy Prescription: Set Healthy Boundaries
            for Yourself and Others*

CHAPTER 7   **JOY INTERRUPTED**   107
            *Joy Prescription: Live Every Day with
            Intention*

Part III

CHAPTER 8 GOING OFF SCRIPT   123
Joy Prescription: Take a Leap of Faith

CHAPTER 9 FINDING MY VOICE   149
*Joy Prescription: Use Your Voice for
What You Believe In*

CHAPTER 10 LIGHTENING UP   163
*Joy Prescription: Explore Your
Creative Side*

CHAPTER 11 SKIN DEEP   179
Joy Prescription: Be Your Authentic Self

CHAPTER 12 IF YOU DON'T LAUGH, YOU'LL CRY   191
Joy Prescription: Find the Funny in Life

Conclusion   205
Acknowledgments   207

INTRODUCTION

HOW I LEARNED TO STOP CHASING PERFECTION AND EMBRACE CONNECTION

THE CLOCK HIT 5 P.M. I CHANGED OUT OF MY SCRUBS AND LEFT the hospital, where I'd been working for the past ten hours as an anesthesiologist. During my drive home, I listened to a podcast at 1.5× speed because squeezing as much as I could out of every second of my day was my modus operandi. I pulled into my garage and turned the volume down, preparing for my "second shift"—or the 5–9, after you work your 9–5. I absolutely adored my children and was excited to see them after a long day at work, but first I needed just five minutes of silence when no one needed me. I put my phone on silent and reclined my seat back.

The next thing I knew, my husband, Daniel, was standing there with my car door open. "Are you okay?" he asked.

Oops, I guess my five minutes turned into thirty.

"Oh my gosh, I must have fallen asleep," I said as I gathered my things and followed him into the house.

There, I was greeted by my twin girls, who ran to give me hugs and kisses. Since I worked full-time, I treasured the little moments that I got to spend with them. When I was home, I wanted to be the one doing everything for and with them. Perhaps this was a subconscious effort to alleviate my guilt for working outside the home.

Daniel cooked dinner while I got on the floor and played with the girls. We always made a point of eating dinner together as a family except for the one night per week that the nanny stayed late and we went out for date night. After dinner, we'd play a family game, or if the weather was nice, we'd go for a walk—a double stroller and three dogs taking up the whole sidewalk. Many nights, after I'd tucked the girls into bed, I'd get on the computer to start my third shift, working on lectures, manuscripts, and grants from 9 p.m. to midnight. When anyone asked how I was doing, I would respond with "fine," "good," or "busy." Life *was* good, but I felt like something was missing. The way I was living, there just wasn't much space for anything else.

One day I was having coffee with a colleague at work. "I just feel like every day is a mad dash to see how many items I can cross off my to-do list," I lamented.

"What happens if you cross everything off?" she asked.

"I don't know. I've never done it before. Every day I'm exhausted, but it seems like I'm not doing enough."

"Maybe you should focus more on your self-care," she suggested.

Self-care? Wasn't that what weak women did when they couldn't handle their lives? *Oh no, not me. I don't need silly self-care. I can keep going.* I was responsible, tough, and capable. Need something done? Give it to me. I wasn't some dainty flower who needed eight hours of sleep or people to pat me on the back and tell me "Good job." The problem, however, was that I ate poorly, slept poorly, and felt poorly. But I was willing to make those sacrifices in order to prove that I was worthy. Recently, I read that self-care needs to be a daily practice and not an emergency procedure. I wish I had learned that much earlier.

I liked my life, but sometimes I wondered how I'd gotten here. I had a gorgeous home that I barely enjoyed. I had a closet full of nice things I bought to soothe myself, but I didn't feel soothed. I had a beautiful family that I didn't spend enough time with. I felt grateful but stuck, successful but disappointed, content but weary. The problem was that I was addicted to the hustle. *Doing* was such an integral part of my being that I could not fathom a life in which I could feel worthy by just *being*.

How would I demonstrate my aptitude, industriousness, and grit if I wasn't out there constantly showing everyone how much I could get done? I was constantly trying to fill the void inside me with achievements, accolades, and accoutrements. I thought, *If I just work harder, I'll be happier.* If I worked hard enough and ran fast enough, perhaps I could outrun the loneliness and sense of worthlessness I felt. But it didn't help. I still felt empty inside.

Because I was constantly chasing perfection, I missed out on many moments of connection, especially with the people closest to me. I still needed to improve my relationship with my mother, which had been built on a fragile foundation since childhood. I wanted to be the best mom I could be for my children, but I felt guilty that on many days I brought home only the shell of the person I wanted to be for them. I loved my career, but I felt torn between being a good doctor and being a good mom, because there didn't seem to be enough time in the day to be both. I was tired, cynical, and snappy. I felt disconnected from the world—as if I were moving through life living on the very surface but never getting deep enough to make any actual meaningful connections. Subconsciously, I was doing this to prevent myself from getting hurt, but it was also preventing me from having true connection with other people—and with myself.

When I had time to sit and think about what was missing, the same thing kept coming to me—joy. *Okay*, I thought, *I've identified the problem. But what's the solution?* I want to make it very clear that I was not unhappy; I just felt like something was missing. I thought that in life, if you worked hard, one day you'd attain a level of success that would fulfill you and make you whole. But it was becoming apparent to me that this was not necessarily true, and I couldn't just keep doing the same thing and expect different results.

I knew that I needed to stop and make myself whole from the inside out.

First, I did all the things that society says you should do to take better care of yourself, like hiring a professional organizer, signing up for a meal delivery service, and going on a yoga retreat. But guess what? None of those things actually did much to make me feel better in the long run. Those things were Band-Aids for the real work that I needed to do, which was to remake myself from the inside out, the way that I truly wanted to, leaving behind the world of comparison, competition, and achievement. I wanted to embrace creativity, connection, and laughter—I wanted to live my life with deeper intention.

All my life, I imagined that I was climbing this great mountain and that there would be a pot of gold waiting for me at the summit. Day after day, I climbed, never resting or deviating from the path. Then one day, when I finally had the chance to stop and take a look around, I couldn't remember why I had wanted to climb this mountain so badly in the first place. I had to stop for a while so I could find clarity on *what* I was doing with my life—and, more importantly, *why* I was doing those things.

Once I figured this out, I stopped living my life on autopilot. I stopped mindlessly trekking up that mountain without questioning whether it was the correct path for me. I also started to look around me and pay attention to my surroundings. Once I did that, I realized that I was learning many lessons along the way and that these lessons would be the key to discovering how I could live my life with more joy.

I started thinking of them as prescriptions—joy prescriptions—on how to truly live for myself. And now I want to pass these joy prescriptions on to you. Maybe you feel like I once did. Maybe you feel stuck in the roles that you've taken on, that you've accepted without question. Maybe you feel trapped by the expectations of those around you and by the pressures of trying to fit into the over-achieving mold, making everyone other than yourself happy. Hopefully, through my story, you'll find that somewhere inside, you have the ability to follow your passions, take that chance, and live your truest, most authentic life.

PART I

CHAPTER 1

CHOOSE YOUR OWN ADVENTURE

Me with my grandparents in Tiananmen Square, age five

'M SIX YEARS OLD, SITTING ALONE ON A PLANE GOING FROM BEIjing to New York City. The flight is long, and sometimes I feel afraid, but there's no one I can talk to, no hand I can hold. My parents aren't there with me—I haven't seen them in two years, since they left me behind in China to pursue a better life for our family in America. I can't remember whether they sneaked out quietly in the middle of the night and I woke up the next morning without them or whether there were protracted hugs, kisses, and tears.

My maternal grandparents, who took care of me in my parents' absence, aren't with me on the plane either. It wouldn't have been easy for them to get visas, nor do they have the money to afford such a trip. For the past two years, I lived with them in their apartment in Harbin, a large city in cold northwestern China. My grandmother and I slept in the same bed every night; she was my best (and only) friend. In the mornings, my grandfather and I went to the market to pick up fresh produce and meat that he cooked for dinner.

When my grandparents told me I was being sent to America to live with my parents, I was devastated. I wanted to stay with them in China. At the airport, a flight attendant had to peel me off my grandmother as I cried and screamed, begging them to take me home.

But now, my new home will be America, a place I know nothing about, and with parents I can hardly remember.

On the flight, the nice flight attendant who's been assigned to look after me asks if I want something to drink.

"I don't have any money," I say.

"It's free," she tells me as she hands me a can of Coca-Cola. "Drink as much as you want."

And so I do. I grip each cold can of Coke for comfort and let the sweet, caffeinated beverage overtake my thoughts.

What will my parents be like?

Where will we live?

I don't know any English ... what will happen to me in school?

Who will fetch Grandpa's slippers when he comes home from work if I'm not there?

I drink six cans of Coke on that flight from China to America. After we land, the flight attendant helps me off the plane, and I spot my parents at the gate. The first thing I say to my mom after two years apart is "我需要尿尿." *I gotta go pee.*

MEMORY IS FUNNY. WHAT IS YOUR EARLIEST MEMORY FROM YOUR childhood? Is it positive or negative, happy or sad? Has it changed over time, or is it different from how someone else remembers the event? If I could summarize how I felt when I first arrived in America in one word, it would be *lonely*. In fact, if I could describe my entire childhood in one word, that word would be *lonely*. That feeling of loneliness has stayed with me into my adult life.

After I landed in America, my parents drove us to their one-bedroom apartment. In many ways, I didn't know my mother and father—I had not seen them for more than two years, and they felt very foreign to me. There was no happy reunion when I joined them—no "I missed you so much" or "Let's go celebrate being together again." They just went back to their school and work, and I started first grade. Mostly, I just missed my grandmother and sleeping in the same bed with her each night. My parents were so busy that I often felt like a burden to them; I felt that their lives were probably easier when I wasn't around. I tried to make myself as small and quiet as possible so as not to further burden or irritate them.

Our apartment was tiny, with no couch, toys, or pets. The living room furniture consisted of a few folding chairs and a folding table my mom had acquired from a garage sale. We didn't even own a television. For fun, I'd look out our front window and watch people use the pay phone on the corner, making up stories in my head about who they were and the conversations they were having. Were these people talking to loved ones they'd been separated from? Were they planning to reunite as I dreamed of doing with my grandparents? Once, someone was taking too long on the phone, and a fight broke out. I watched in fascination, wondering what urgent matter needed to be discussed. Another time, in the middle of the night when we were all asleep, there was a drive-by shooting that put a bullet through our front window. Fortunately, no one was hurt, but I remember staring at the broken glass and thinking it must have been the police chasing a bad guy. As only the police and military had guns in China, I didn't know that ordinary people were allowed to have guns here in America.

In our apartment, my parents had the only bedroom, and "my room" was the living room. (I didn't get my own room until we moved to a house when I was ten.) I slept on a twin-size mattress on the floor without a box spring or bed frame. This was my first time sleeping alone, since back in China, I'd shared my grandmother's bed. I don't know whether it was the trauma of moving and being away from my grandparents or the new environment, but I often woke up to find the mattress beneath me soaking wet. I was so ashamed the first few times it happened that I didn't say anything and just covered it up, trying to use extra blankets at night because the mattress underneath was still wet.

Have you ever tried to wash urine out of a mattress? Completely out? You can't. No matter how hard my mom tried to scrub it away, the smell of urine remained.

My dad was furious and would yell at me, "How are you wetting the bed? You're six years old. This is so shameful! You're ruining the mattress we bought for you!"

I sat there with tears streaming down my face and said, "Sorry, Baba, I'll try to stop."

"Stop crying. You're a disgrace."

My dad continued to berate me, and then one morning, a few months later and for no apparent reason, I just stopped. To this day, my dad likes to take credit for putting a stop to my bed-wetting problem. *See, if I hadn't yelled at you, you'd probably have wet the bed much longer.* (Right, Dad, I probably would have peed my top bunk bed in college, and it would have dripped onto my poor roommate sleeping below.)

I started first grade in the middle of the school year, not knowing a lick of English. Because I couldn't tell the difference between the words *boys* and *girls*, I went into the wrong bathroom on my first day. When I looked up and saw a bunch of boys pointing and laughing at me, I realized my mistake and ran out, mortified. I was put into an English as a second language (ESL) classroom, where most of the other kids spoke Spanish. I learned about as much Spanish as I did English in those early months of school, but I didn't know what was what—I was just learning new words.

Before I could even finish first grade, we moved to a different neighborhood and I started at a new school. This would happen again and again throughout my childhood, with my family moving every year or two and me going to many different schools. I got used to being the new girl and having few friends. Overall, I ended up attending three elementary schools, two middle schools, and two high schools. I was never consulted about these decisions. My parents would announce the week before that we were moving, and then it would happen. It was like being a military kid but much less cool. Every time we moved, it was because one of my parents had gotten a better job, and as we climbed another rung on the socioeconomic ladder, we were able to afford a slightly nicer apartment in a better neighborhood.

When I first arrived in America, my dad was going to school full-time to get his master's in computer science. Since he was on a student visa, he wasn't technically supposed to be working, but he found a Chinese restaurant that let him wash dishes in the back for two dollars an hour. He was either in school, studying, or working. During that time, my mom was the main breadwinner of the house, working as a receptionist at an insurance company. Because my parents were so busy, I learned the skills of independence and responsibility from an early age. I woke myself up, ate Pop-Tarts or cereal for breakfast, rode the bus both ways to school, and was the quintessential latchkey kid. The rules were to come home right after school, not to answer the door, and to make sure to finish my homework before my parents got home. During the week, I didn't see my parents much except at dinnertime. Sometimes after dinner, if my father was in a good mood, we would play Chinese checkers or cards. Then they'd retreat to their bedroom to work and I'd stay in my room (the living room), reading until I fell asleep.

After completing my homework, which I *always* did, I read. A lot. The highlight of my week was going to the public library on Saturdays with my mom to check out new books—I could read twenty books in a single week. To me, these books showed what life could be like in America. From Nancy Drew, I learned what it was like to be brave in the face of danger; from the Baby-Sitters Club and the Sweet Valley High series, I learned what it was like to have friends, talk to boys, and have sleepovers.

My favorite series, however, was Choose Your Own Adventure. I loved the excitement of these stories, with the characters getting to decide whether to take this road or that road, keep going or turn back. Lying in my bed at night, I would turn the pages and imagine a different existence for myself, one in which I could make my own choices:

> If you decide to stay in China, turn to page **8**.
> If you decide to go to America, turn to page **13**.

The reality of my life was anything but adventurous, and I had very little choice in anything that I did. I hadn't chosen to come to America. I hadn't chosen to move and change schools every couple of years. I certainly hadn't chosen my parents. When I read these books, though, I felt like I had a sense of control over my life, and I got a glimpse of the possibilities it could offer.

I would read until I fell asleep, sometimes with the book still open and my hand holding my place as if I planned to pick up where I left off when I awoke. Reading helped me to escape the mundanity and loneliness of my life. To this day, just turning the pages of a book—the smell of a book—has the power to transport me to another world.

Making new friends every time we moved felt impossible, and I felt like books were my only companions. I was also shy and awkward as a kid, preferring to hang out with just one or two other girls at a time instead of a larger group. On top of that, my parents didn't trust anyone, so I wasn't allowed to have playdates at friends' houses. Sometimes a friend came to our house, usually under the guise of needing to "study" together, but even in those cases, things often did not go as planned.

Once when I had a friend over, I asked her if she wanted to stay for dinner, and to my astonishment, she said yes. That night, my mom steamed a whole fish for dinner. When she set it in the middle of the table, my friend exclaimed, "Gross, what is it? Is that an eyeball?" I guess her family didn't eat a lot of fresh seafood at home. She decided to share her experience with the other kids at school, and by Monday afternoon, everyone was calling me "Fish Face." I never invited anyone to stay for dinner after that.

At school, I was learning a lot of new words, some of which were not so nice. I was called a Ch**k, Slanty Eyes, Ching Chong...you name it, I've probably been called it. Lunch and recess were the worst. At least during class time, the teacher would be talking or we'd be working on an assignment. That gave me something to do. But at lunch, I had no one to sit with, and that deep feeling of loneliness returned. Recess was even worse. I had no one to play with, and I would wander around, trying to look like I belonged or just picking flowers and daydreaming. I couldn't wait for the bell to ring and for class to start again.

One day a group of kids approached me on the playground and asked me to play with them.

Me? I looked around to make sure they weren't talking to someone else.

Yeah, you, they said. *Come play with us.*

So a few of us jumped on the merry-go-round while the others spun it. It wasn't really my cup of tea, but I wasn't about to miss this chance to make some friends. Suddenly all the other kids jumped off the merry-go-round, leaving me spinning on my own as they made it go faster and faster. I clenched the handlebar, trying to keep my footing. The world was spinning so fast that I felt like my stomach was going to come out of my mouth. "*Stop, stop, stop,*" I cried. By the time a teacher heard me and came over to stop the merry-go-round, tears were streaming down my face and urine was streaming down my legs. (Again, the smell of hot pee.)

Things weren't any easier by third grade, when I learned that I had to get glasses. (Must have been all that reading under the covers with a flashlight.) One day in gym class, they fell off my face as I was running. The kid behind me deliberately stepped on them and smashed them. When my mom got home from work that day, I handed her the broken frames. Before I even had a chance to explain, she yelled, "*Aiya*, Tiffany, how can you be so careless? These cost a lot of money!"

When my dad got home, I explained to him what had happened. "People at school are calling me names and being mean," I told him. "They broke my glasses on purpose and then laughed."

Nowadays a parent might respond with something like *They're just words* or *It's okay, we love you*. A really evolved parent might even take the time to have a conversation with their child about how the mean names made them feel. But my dad's response was "Study more and work harder. When you're older, you will have a better job and make more money than any of those idiots, and that will be your revenge," which in retrospect was kind of a dark thing to tell an eight-year-old.

After a while, I gave up on telling my parents that I was being bullied at school. What was the use? They only wanted to hear that I was getting good grades and not getting into any trouble. I felt that they were not open to another kind of parent-child relationship with me, one in which I was free to express my thoughts and fears and could be heard and seen. And contrary to what my dad's advice implied, bullying is not confined to childhood. It doesn't stop just because you are an adult and have a decent job.

It didn't occur to me until much later that my dad probably experienced bullying and discrimination himself. I was too busy dealing with my own bullies to think that maybe he had bullies too. Maybe he'd even been called some of the same names I'd been called. (I guess bullies aren't all that creative when it comes to name-calling.) Of course we never talked about this, but it was something I sensed. My dad always had a chip on his shoulder about Americans—how wasteful they were, how uneducated many were, and how they spoke only one language. I think this was his way of coping with how difficult life was in America. It wasn't until decades later that I learned that in China, my father had been the manager of a large factory and had overseen hundreds of employees. He initially came to America to study business management, but his lack of English skills made it so difficult that he switched his degree to computer science so he wouldn't have to talk to other people. *How sad*, I thought. *No wonder he has a chip on his shoulder.*

Thank goodness you didn't need to understand English to be good at math. When I started school in America, even though I didn't speak English, I was already a grade ahead in math. Throughout elementary school, I was always the first one in my class to finish math tests, and I usually got perfect scores. My classmates would try to cheat off me. *Math was my jam.* At home, my dad always gave me extra math worksheets. Since I didn't have many friends, I didn't know this wasn't a normal extracurricular activity. (Wait, you mean to tell me not everyone goes home after school and does ten extra pages of math worksheets?) Nor did I know that it wasn't normal for parents to make their kids stay up late at night to finish their work. My dad had a simple rule for math homework—for every *question* I got wrong, he would make me do one more *sheet* of math problems. I guess he was extrapolating from "An eye for an eye" to "A page for a problem."

Once, he gave me a sheet of math problems involving fractions or something that my brain couldn't figure out. "Why don't you understand?" he yelled. "It's not that difficult. Are you stupid?" And he set down another sheet of math problems in front of me.

That night I stayed up until 3 a.m. because I kept getting questions wrong. Around midnight my mom tried to step in and said to my dad, "She's only nine; let her go to sleep." Tiger Dad wouldn't have any of that, though—he gave her a look, and she silently retreated to her bedroom. The next day I was delirious and spent lunch and recess with my head propped against the wall in the last bathroom stall, napping until the bell rang.

Today I understand that my dad was so hard on me because he believed that academic success would lead to financial success and that financial success was the key to making it in America. Both of my parents had that tunnel vision throughout their lives. They still do, to be honest—which is not that uncommon for anyone who's immigrated to this country.

But as a kid, I didn't see that. All I saw were endless pages of math problems, my parents always working and never enjoying themselves, and their constant fighting about money.

ARE THERE BELIEFS THAT YOUR PARENTS PASSED DOWN THAT YOU never questioned until you grew up? It might be where you're supposed to live, what kind of job you should have, or whom you should hang out with. My parents had strict ideas of what success meant and what would make you happy in life. They never said that money equals happiness, but I could tell from their actions that money was important and that a *lack* of money could make you quite unhappy.

If saving money were an Olympic sport, my mom would have more gold medals than Michael Phelps. On Mondays after she got off work, she'd stop by the local rec center, where the Sunday paper had been thrown out, and pull out the glossy coupon section. I waited eagerly for her to come home. It was my job to clip the coupons and arrange them in order of how they'd be used, according to the layout of the grocery store, so that we could be efficient in our quest to save. I had a very good memory and knew the exact order of the aisles at the grocery store where we shopped: aisle 1 was canned goods and soups, aisle 2 (which we almost never went to) was candy and baking supplies, aisle 3 was cereal and juices, and so on.

Tuesday was double-coupon day. After my mom got off work, we would go to the grocery store and make a game of finding the correct items, aisle by aisle. I had to have an eye for detail because the coupons had certain caveats, like specific item sizes and flavors you had to purchase, in order to work. But sometimes, when we played it right, we could basically get items for free. *And nothing tastes better than free!* (Or so I thought.)

Another important part of the grocery store was the area of the produce section with discounted fruit—fruit that was bruised or starting to rot.

Once my mom picked up a small bag of apples and said, "See, Tiffany? I can buy this whole bag for fifty cents. If I bought apples from the regular section, they'd be several dollars."

"But this one is rotten," I pointed out.

My mom glanced at the apples. "That can be fixed."

And when we got home, she cut the rotten part out of the apple and handed the rest of it to me. I bit into it, and she was right—it was perfectly tasty. I was proud that my mom was so resourceful and that I was her little helper.

If there was money left over after grocery shopping, my mom might let me get a treat at the checkout counter. I've never been a big candy or chocolate person, but I loved gum—my favorite was the fruity kind with a zebra on the package. In order to be frugal, I would sometimes chew just half a stick. Other times I would stick my gum on the corner of the dining room table, saving it for later. Only after two or three chews, when the gum was completely taste-less and hard as a rock, would I have the heart to throw it out. Help-ing my mom save money made me feel like I was contributing to the family and earning my keep. At times I felt like I was a burden to my parents as an extra mouth to feed, so I wanted to show that I could pull my own weight.

My mom was also a master bargainer. At the markets where she shopped in China, you always bargained to buy something. It was expected—only a fool would pay the asking price for something. My mom brought this skill with her to America. On Saturday mornings, we'd wake up early and drive around the neighborhood to check out all the garage sales. Everything we owned—our furniture, dishes, and clothes—was carefully curated from these lawn displays of other people's unwanted items.

One time my mom pointed to a stack of mismatched dishes that were marked $5 and said, "Tiffany, watch how I can get these for less."

She approached the owner of the house. "Excuse me, these dishes...some are chipped...I give you one dollar."

"Ma'am, how about I give them to you for three dollars?" the man suggested.

"One dollar." My mom was firm.

The man scratched his head and looked at her, this tiny Asian woman standing her ground. I took a chipped plate and held it out for the man to see.

"Okay, fine, one dollar," he acquiesced.

I could tell that my mom gloated inside every time we ate off those dishes.

My mom still has no shame in her bargaining game. Years ago, when I took her shopping for a dress to wear to my wedding, she found a beautiful red dress, but the only one in her size had some loose beads at the bottom.

As we approached the cash register, I said to her, "Let's ask if they have another one in the back."

Mom had a different idea. "I want to buy this dress, but you see—there are some loose beads at the bottom. Can you give us a discount?" she asked the sales associate.

My face flushed the same color as the dress—I had no idea my mom was going to ask for a discount at this high-end department store.

"Sure, I can take 10 percent off," the cashier said.

My mom looked at me and smiled. She was saving money, even though it wasn't even *her* money. Later, at home, she resewed the loose beads onto the dress.

As a child, I came to understand that sense of pride my mom must have felt each time she saved money. When she bought me a Barbie doll for a dollar, and later I saw a similar, though new, version in a store for ten dollars, I'd think, *We're outsmarting the system.* It echoed my dad's belief that Americans were wasteful and that we could do better.

Although I knew we were poor, I never got the sense that this was intrinsically bad or shameful—until other people made me feel bad about it. Kids at school would tease me, saying things like "Do you shop at Goodwill or something?" and "Your jeans have holes in them." (This was before it was cool to have jeans with holes in them.) Most of my clothes were secondhand, and I seldom had new shoes. Once, though, after I got straight A's for the entire year, my mom took me to Payless shoe store and bought me a brand-new pair of shoes—see-through pink glitter Jellies. I loved those shoes (you can say my obsession with footwear started at an early age).

Since money was tight, I didn't have many possessions, but I did have an affinity for office supplies. I would collect pens, pencils, erasers, notebooks, and stickers, which I kept inside a Hello Kitty pencil case—never to be used, only to be occasionally taken out and admired as if they were precious baseball cards. My mom sometimes bought me dolls or stuffed animals, but if my dad found out, he would yell at her for wasting money. Many of my parents' fights were about money. He would ask her why the grocery bill was so high, and she would try to calm him down. Sometimes she would argue with him, but that only seemed to infuriate him more. I remember lying on my mattress in the living room at night, listening to his voice rising higher and higher in their bedroom.

That night, I made a promise to myself: *When I grow up, I'm going to work so hard that I don't ever have to worry about money.* To an extent, that came true. But these are two sides of the same coin: although I am financially secure and don't have to worry about money, frugality is forever ingrained in me. Like my mom, I live for a deal, and while I may not buy the bruised and half-rotten produce,

I do generally buy whatever fruit is on sale (also because it tends to be what's in season and freshest).

For better or worse, my parents taught me that money was important. They also taught me that money can be an incessant source of conflict. I know now that while money can smooth your path—can make your journey more comfortable—it can't completely protect you from the shadows along the way. Sometimes it can even make it harder for you to figure out just what light you're moving toward.

⌒

WHEN I WAS TEN, WE MOVED INTO A HOUSE IN A SUBURB OF Dallas. It was a real freestanding house, not an apartment where we shared walls with another family or had noisy neighbors stomping on the ceiling. Two thousand square feet to call our own. There was a driveway with a two-car garage where my parents could park their cars. Best of all, I would finally have my own bedroom.

My parents were so proud when they took me to see our new house for the first time. Standing with them in the doorway, even before taking a step inside, I felt proud too. Through my coupon clipping and endless saving, my sacrifice of playing with used toys and wearing used clothes, I had helped them afford an actual house. I finally understood why my parents had worked so hard and why they had brought me to America. I understood the American Dream.

Mom and Dad are right, I thought as I stared at our house. *I should complain less.*

This was what they had been working so hard for, what they meant when they told me that I needed to work even harder than they did so that I could get a good job when I grew up. I know they did all this out of love for me and the hope that I would have a better life. But at what price? Growing up, I never felt that the love my parents had for me was unconditional. They would often say things like "If it weren't for you, we would have just stayed in China. We came here and dealt with the challenges of learning a new language and being in an unfamiliar country in order to give *you* the opportunity for a better life." Other times they'd say, "You better take care of us when we're old. You owe it to us." Looking back, I realize that was a lot of pressure to put on a kid. Much of my life has centered on trying to please them, make them proud, and show them that their sacrifices have been worthwhile.

I never expected my parents to give me a picture-perfect childhood. I just wish everything didn't always have to be so hard with them. I also understand that a large part of my success in life is a by-product of the sacrifices they made and the values that they instilled in me when I was growing up. It pains me to realize that *because* my parents were toiling away to achieve the American Dream, they were not able to give me the ideal American childhood, complete with family vacations, after-school activities, and their time and attention. Their lives did not involve a lot of choice or adventure either. And what I have come to realize today, with some time and perspective (and lots of therapy), is that they sacrificed so that I would have the freedom to pursue my own dreams.

We are all a combination of our pasts, our present lives, and the decisions we make for ourselves that will drive us into the future. We can't erase the past, but we can make peace with what has happened to us while acknowledging both sides of the equation. For me, this means learning to accept and embrace two opposing emotions: my gratitude to my parents for their sacrifices to give our family a better life in America and the pain of feeling lonely and neglected as a child. My parents did the best they could with what they had, bringing me up according to the way they had been raised and with the cultural values that they had brought over from China. They put food on the table, kept me warm and clothed, and gave me an education. To them, that was good parenting.

When people ask me if I had a happy or sad childhood, I don't know how to answer because the truth is that it was both. My memories of my dad scolding me for wetting the bed or getting a math question wrong sit right next to the ones of him chasing me around the house or taking me fishing. These stories and emotions can coexist because they are human stories. We are all human, and we are all full of contradictions.

The feelings of loneliness that defined my childhood will probably stay with me throughout my life. However, I can use the memory of that feeling to shape the way I live and to make conscious choices in my own life. For example, because I don't have to struggle to feed and clothe my kids, I can choose to be a different kind of parent to them. I can also talk to my parents about the things that happened in my childhood without blaming them.

Maybe you had a happy childhood. If so, congratulations! You can take the thousands of dollars that you would have spent on therapy and go on vacation. But maybe it's not that easy. Maybe you have issues stemming from the way you grew up, and you're going to have to do the work to move forward.

Of course, if you are really struggling, don't be afraid to seek out professional help. Personally, I have seen a therapist to untangle my complicated thoughts and feelings about my own childhood, and it has helped clarify many things for me. When you do the work of confronting painful memories from your past, you empower yourself by taking ownership of those memories and acknowledging them in all their complexity. You can honor them before letting them go. This will free you to choose your own adventure and to go wherever your heart takes you.

JOY PRESCRIPTION

Let Go of the Past

- *Honor your truth, but respect others' interpretations.* Family members often feel differently about the same situation. Because our individual interpretations of events differ, our feelings regarding those events may differ as well. How you feel is your truth, but also be open for others to share their truth.

- *Identify the feelings you associate with the event and validate them.* Even if your memory of an event doesn't match up with what your family member recalls, the effect that it has had on your life is real and should be acknowledged.

- *Think about how the events have shaped you in a positive way.* Instead of dwelling on the past, focus on the outcome. Consider how the events have affected your life and shaped your personality. For example, has adversity made you more resourceful? Did having less means growing up make you more grateful for your financial security? You may not be able to change the past, but you can take what you've learned from it to create a better future.

CHAPTER 2

COMPARE AND CONTRAST

Me, age eleven, with baby Josh

THERE ARE SOME UNIVERSAL TRUTHS IN AN ASIAN HOUSEHOLD. Shoes must never be worn inside the house. The dishwasher is used only as a drying rack. A paper towel must be used multiple times before it can be thrown away. And perhaps the most important one of all: no matter how smart and obedient you are, your parents will know of someone else's child who is even smarter and more obedient, *and they will constantly compare you to them.*

When I was growing up, competition was the norm for my family. My parents attended a nearby Chinese Baptist church—not because they were particularly religious but for the social and community aspects. Plus, church was where they competed in their favorite sport—bragging about the accomplishments of their children. Often this would be disguised as complaining—"*Aiya*, Tiffany make straight A's on her report card this year, but she cannot play any music instrument. Your Sarah is such a good daughter, make good grade and play both piano and violin!" Usually this was said in front of us kids as if we weren't standing right there, listening to every word. Everything seemed like a competition.

Have you ever been unable to enjoy something because you were constantly comparing yourself to someone else? And then you start focusing on what the other person is doing instead of what you're supposed to be doing? That way of thinking has never sat right with me. It's like getting a slice of cake and focusing on the fact that someone else got a bigger slice instead of just enjoying your own cake. All this does is foster a sense that life is a competition, that everything is win-lose, and that you need to do everything you can to be a winner.

To some extent, my parents' attitude toward competition made sense. In China, it was a rare privilege to get an education. In my dad's rural village, only 1 percent of the high school students passed the entrance examination for college. Then my parents had to compete with thousands of other Chinese students to get student visas in order to study in America. So it made sense that they would see their lives in a new country as a continuation of that scarcity, always stretching every dollar, optimizing any opportunity, and criticizing anything below perfection. The result, however, was that I never felt good enough.

While many of my peers faced the added pressure of being compared to their siblings, I didn't have to worry about that since I was an only child. I'd always wanted a little brother or sister, someone I could play with so that I didn't have to make imaginary friends or pretend my dolls could talk back to me. But when my mom's friends said to her, "Your daughter is so obedient and smart. You should have another one," my mom's answer was always "No, no more children for me."

So imagine my shock when one day, when I was ten, my mom told me matter-of-factly that I was going to have a baby brother. *What?* After I'd wished for a sibling all those years and finally given up? *Now* I was going to have a baby brother? Well, I didn't want one anymore. *It's too late*, I thought pessimistically.

Ask two siblings what their childhoods were like, and you may get two totally opposite experiences. Siblings can describe their parents in completely different ways, and they may both be right. I always say to my brother, Josh, "We had different parents," to which he'll say, "That's ridiculous; we have the same parents." Genetically, yes. But in every other way—not so much. By the time Josh was born, eleven years after me, our parents were more financially stable. He never had to live in a tiny apartment with noisy upstairs neighbors or change schools every few years, and he always had his own room. His toys and clothes were bought new—no trucks with missing parts or ill-fitting hand-me-downs for him.

By the time Josh was born, my parents had also adopted some Western ways of living. For example, instead of getting their furniture from garage sales, they went to Rooms To Go and purchased a living room set that actually matched. Sure, they kept the plastic cover on the couch (another universal truth in an Asian household) so that the couch made a crinkly sound when you sat on it, but it was a start.

Before my brother came along, we never went on vacations and hardly ever went out to eat besides the occasional fast-food joint, but now my parents were going to sit-down restaurants. Our favorite place was the Olive Garden (which my mom called "Oliver

Garden"). The rules, however, were that we could order only water (don't even *think* about ordering a soda), eat as much of the free breadsticks and salad as we could, and then order two entrees to be split among the four of us and take the leftovers home.

Now, at the grocery store, my mom no longer bought half-rotten fruit and instead stressed the importance of buying only organic strawberries because pesticides were dangerous. I thought, *Who are you, and what have you done with my mother?* While part of me was happy that Josh didn't have to endure the same hardships I had, another part of me felt a little bitter. Once, he received a Nintendo for his birthday—something I'd begged my parents for when I was younger. They had proclaimed that video games were doubly evil because they not only cost money but also rotted your brain. Instead, I should go read a book or do extra math worksheets. There was no way a gaming console was going to make it into our household. Then, lo and behold, ten years later, my brother was squirming around on the plastic-covered living room sofa, which crinkled away as he played *Super Mario*. I was so angry.

"You know you don't have to duck when your character ducks, right? You look stupid," I said to him.

"You're just jealous," he retorted.

Why, yes, I was jealous. My inner eight-year-old was crying at the unfairness of it all.

I sometimes worried that Josh had it too easy and that he was being spoiled. I mean, how would he grow up to have perseverance and grit if he never had to cut off the bad part of an apple before eating it? He used entire sticks of gum and threw them away after just one chew. He wouldn't know what it was like being a latchkey kid or never having friends because of moving schools all the time. Mostly I was concerned that Josh would lack the skills I had learned from growing up in a tough household—to be frugal, work hard, and make personal sacrifices. How would he develop the fortitude to deal with life's challenges when everything had been handed to him on a silver platter? What if he was too soft for this world? (Spoiler alert: he turned out just fine.)

Around age twelve, I started to make some friends because I was able to spend more than a year at the same school. I was invited to go to the movies and the mall, but my parents wouldn't let me. Instead, I had to stay home and watch Josh while they were working. After all, it was free babysitting for them.

When I objected, my dad would say, "You're a part of this family. You live here; you eat our food. We're just asking you to contribute by watching your little brother. And you want to go hang out with your friends? Who are these friends? Do they even care about you? Trust me, in ten years, you won't even remember their names. But this is your family, and you have an obligation to us." And so on. My dad never lectured for ten minutes when he could lecture for thirty. The end result was that I went from being upset because I couldn't go to the mall to feeling guilty. Guilt, resentment, and fear were my predominant feelings about my father. His temper was unpredictable, and he could go from slightly annoyed to enraged if I talked back, so I generally acquiesced to his lecturing so that he would slide back toward annoyance rather than fury.

Then there was the matter of sleepovers. I was so excited when I got invited to my first sleepover, which until then I'd only read about in books. "Absolutely not," my father said. I tried to explain to him that if I didn't go, I would miss out on not only what happened *at* the sleepover but all the conversations the girls would have about it *afterward* (basically I was trying to explain that he was ruining my life). Still, he wouldn't budge. At lunch on Monday, all the girls were giggling about how they had used *67 to prank-call boys. I felt confused and out of the loop. Each time I got invited, I would ask my parents if I could go, but they always said no. They didn't know the other parents, and they didn't want me spending the night at a stranger's house. After a while, I stopped asking because I already knew what the answer would be. To this day, sleepovers remain the elusive symbol of friendship to me because I didn't have them growing up.

My parents' immigrant mentality meant that not only could they not trust other people, but they couldn't even trust their own daughter. It wasn't as if, had I been allowed to go to the mall, I would have smoked cigarettes and made out with boys (not that any boys wanted to make out with me). All I wanted to do was have fun with my friends, to do what typical American teenagers did. But that wasn't something my parents could understand. Their MO was to study more, work harder, and be better. As a result, my early teenage life was a closed circuit of home, school, and then home again to take care of my brother and study. I was starting to feel trapped, literally and figuratively, in the prison of my parents' house.

None of this was Josh's fault, of course. He was just a little kid. I had wanted a sibling so badly during all those years when I'd been lonely and playing with my imaginary friends. Just when I'd given up on ever having a playmate, my parents had sprung this on me. It seemed like a cruel joke. Yet today, when I tell Josh how I felt that our parents were much easier on him, he brings up how they always compared him to me, and he felt like he had big shoes to fill.

At your age, your sister did twenty math sheets a night.

You got a B? Your sister never got a B!

At your age, your sister was so mature and independent. Why can't you be more like your sister?

I guess I never really saw it that way. In the end, comparison— whether it's between peers or siblings—truly is, as they say, the thief of joy.

THE BIGGEST BRAGGING RIGHTS AMONG MY PARENTS AND THEIR Chinese friends at church was if your kid got into a program called TAMS—the Texas Academy of Mathematics and Science. My mom would always say something like "You know Auntie May's daughter? She got a perfect SAT score and just got accepted to TAMS."

TAMS basically allowed you to skip the last two years of high school and attend college early. It was highly competitive, with only two hundred students selected from high schools across Texas. They also gave you a free ride, and there was no word in the English language my parents loved more than *free*. Having your kid get into TAMS was like the holy trifecta of Asian parenthood—my parents could save money, accelerate my path to becoming a doctor, *and* brag to their friends. It was a given that I would apply. Failure was *not* an option. But rather than seeing TAMS as a necessary stepping stone to success, the way my parents did, I saw it as my ticket to freedom.

Essentially, I applied for college at the age of fourteen. I took the SATs for the second time (I'd already taken them once when I was twelve). I got my letters of recommendation lined up. I wrote a few essays and visited the campus for some interviews. All of this so that I could get a jump start on becoming a doctor so I could make my parents proud.

While my parents embedded the idea of becoming a doctor in me from a young age, I don't remember ever *not* wanting to be a doctor. I had been fascinated by math and science for as long as I could remember. Most of all, I wanted to help people—to make them feel better, to make a difference, and to feel worthy. Both my parents and I were excited the day the TAMS acceptance letter came in the mail, but for different reasons. They were happy to accelerate my path to becoming the first doctor in our family, and I was excited to be getting out of their house.

So, at the ripe age of fifteen, I moved out of my parents' house with a few boxes full of my personal belongings and into the dorm at TAMS.

In the acceptance packet was a questionnaire I filled out about things like sleep habits, music preferences, and hobbies, which was supposed to help them match me up with a roommate. When I was matched with a girl named Vanessa, I thought there must have been some mix-up with my questionnaire. I expected my roommate to be a quiet, nerdy Asian girl just like me, but Vanessa was a Latina with sophistication and spice. We actually met up at a mall in Dallas before the first week of school. It was supposed to be a little get-to-know-you session, but the first thing I did was pull out my notebook and pen and ask her, "What color is your comforter?"

"Ummm, it's gray on one side and purple on the other," Vanessa replied, amused.

"I think it would be better if you left it on the gray side," I informed her. "Purple doesn't really match the leopard theme that I'm going with."

At the time, I was going through an animal-print phase and wanted everything I owned to be leopard print. While my mother hadn't congratulated me on getting into TAMS, she had said, "Let's go to Bed Bath and Beyond and buy you new bedding for your dorm." I knew that was her way of saying she was proud of me. We bought the "bed in a bag" for sixty dollars, which was a *lot* of money back then (and that was after the 20 percent off coupon). It came with a pillowcase, sheets, and a comforter—all in leopard print. I had never slept on new or matching sheets before. I was starting my new life, and I was going to do it in style.

After determining the interior decor of our dorm room, I went on to ask Vanessa whether she preferred the top or bottom bunk, if she was going to supply the minifridge or the microwave, how many boxes she was bringing, and the exact time she was moving in. I had an actual checklist of questions that I went through with her. Fortunately, Vanessa was unbothered and not put off by the little Chinese girl who walked in and started grilling her about what her comforter looked like. Nowadays, when we reminisce about this first meeting, she says, "Girl, I thought you were crazy. I almost asked to change roommates." Thank goodness she didn't.

Vanessa was also from the Dallas area, but in contrast to my sheltered childhood, her upbringing had been vibrant, sophisticated, and cheerful. Her father was from Mexico and her mother from Spain, and she had gone to an international school in Spain. She had traveled throughout Europe and even had a boyfriend. On weekends she had gone out with her friends and sneaked into night clubs while I had been stuck at home reading, doing homework, and looking after my little brother. I giggled as she described to me what it was like to French-kiss a boy—"Oh my gosh, so like you just let him stick his tongue in your mouth? Is it slimy?" There was a lot I needed to catch up on.

To this day, I call Vanessa my "sister from another mister." She was the first person in my life who taught me that I could have fun and still be smart and studious—that the two were not mutually exclusive. That may seem like common sense now, but I promise you, back then it was not. My parents had always acted like a person could either be at home studying and resting or out past 10 p.m. shooting up drugs and stealing cars. I was raised to believe that being studious and successful was the polar opposite of having fun. *I had no idea you could do both.*

Vanessa and I were inseparable, in the dorm and outside it. I had never had a sleepover before, and now I was on a sleepover that never ended. The dorm curfew was 10 p.m. on weekdays and 1 a.m. on weekends. As long as I got good grades, my parents didn't really ask much about what else I was doing. I guess they just assumed I was studying all the time, like I had when I'd lived at home. This was when I first learned about time management. I discovered that as long as I went to class, paid attention, and studied, there was more than enough time to go out and do fun things. Vanessa and I had our fair share of teenage antics, but nothing crazy that would end up with us on *Girls Gone Wild* tapes. We kept it in check.

Although I lived thirty minutes away, I saw my parents only during the holiday break. Those two weeks at home were like torture for me. At TAMS I was hanging out with friends and staying up late while making a 4.0 GPA; at home I was back to babysitting my brother and living by my parents' strict rules. I missed Vanessa, my classmates, and the freedom of my new life. I had become a different person and felt confined by my parents' lack of awareness that I was growing.

Most of the time, Vanessa was the one teaching me about new things. However, there was one thing she had never tried before—kimchi. We had a meal plan, but the cafeteria closed at a certain time, and after that, we had to fend for ourselves. We'd buy instant ramen (four cups for a dollar on sale due to my penny-pinching skills) and keep them for when we were up late studying. I also bought a small jar of kimchi from a Korean grocery store and kept it in our minifridge. After I heated up the ramen in our microwave, I'd peel back the paper and stir in a few pieces of kimchi to improve the flavor of the noodles.

The first time I did this, Vanessa said, "Ewww, Tiff, what *is* that? It smells like farts. Did you fart?"

"It's kimchi—spicy Korean pickled cabbage," I explained and held out my chopsticks to her. "Do you want to try it?"

After taking a hesitant bite, Vanessa's eyes lit up. "That's good!" Years later, she introduced kimchi to her husband, and to this day, she always keeps a jar of it in her fridge.

Some of my favorite memories from this time are our late-night dance parties. We'd be up doing calculus homework until 1 or 2 a.m., so tired that we were doing the head jerk—you know, where your head falls forward and you jerk awake.

"I can't do this," I said to Vanessa. "I can't stay up any longer."

"Let's get up and dance," she suggested. "If you dance a little, your blood will get moving and it'll wake you up."

She put on our favorite songs, "Shake It Fast" by Mystikal and "Back That Azz Up" by Juvenile. Trying to look like I knew what I was doing, I moved my hips from side to side, channeling my inner Shakira. Her hips don't lie, but mine sure did.

"Where did you learn how to dance?" Vanessa asked, laughing.

"Ummm, I didn't," I said, not wanting to admit that I was trying to imitate the MTV music videos I sneak-watched back home when I was babysitting my brother and my parents weren't around.

"Well, your dancing is atrocious. I'll teach you how to really dance." She opened the closet door, where we had hung a mirror, and said, "Watch me. Throw your butt back like this. Uh-huh, that's better. Okay, now speed it up." And just like that, I learned to twerk in a dorm room at 1 a.m. while taking a break from studying calculus.

Of course I also learned a lot of academic things at TAMS. In high school, I had been able to walk into math class having looked at the textbook only ten minutes beforehand and ace the test. Here, I took college-level calculus. I worked in a developmental physiology lab, researching vascular development and angiogenesis in chicken embryos. I signed up with a local organization that mentored kids in underprivileged neighborhoods and went once a week to help them with homework and read with them. I started dating a boy and no longer wondered if tongues were slimy. It was all eye-opening in the best way.

For the first time in my life, I was being challenged, in school and in my personal life. I was beginning to blossom outside the confines of competition and comparison that my parents had always imposed on me. Now, even though I was in the most cutthroat environment I'd ever been in in my life—among two hundred of the most gifted and talented kids in the state—I didn't feel like I had to be better than anyone else. Instead, I felt like I had a real friend in Vanessa, and I was growing in ways I'd never expected. I hadn't realized until then how much I'd been held back by my upbringing and how little I truly knew myself. This taste of freedom was so sweet that I never wanted it to end.

Would I recommend sending your child away to start college at the age of fifteen? Probably not. However, because of the way I had been brought up, it was necessary for me to see that there was more to life than family, school, and studying. It allowed me to realize my potential and to learn that being studious and having fun are not mutually exclusive.

When Josh was a high school sophomore and deciding if he should apply to TAMS, my parents and I encouraged him *not* to. We didn't think he would do well with the freedom and that it would be better for him to stay at home until he matured a bit more. I'm glad that Josh wasn't as mature and independent as I was at that age because it meant he didn't need to be. He had been able to grow up as a kid should, having sleepovers with friends, participating in sports, and playing video games. Most of all, Josh *wanted* to stay home for the last two years of high school because he enjoyed life with my parents. He didn't feel the same desperation to get away from them, because they treated him differently, because by then they were different parents (and people) than they had been with me. And I was happy for him that he didn't want to leave home early.

I don't know if my parents will ever stop comparing me to Josh or comparing the two of us to their friends' kids. The older I get, the higher the stakes seem to become. Instead of comparing grades and SAT scores, there are other metrics.

My mom recently said to me, "You know Auntie Sue's son? He went to Harvard Business School and sold his company for three hundred million dollars."

"Wow, that's amazing. Auntie Sue must be so proud of him," I replied with a mix of admiration and resentment—resentment that my mom never sounded that proud of me.

Perhaps my mom realized this because she quickly added, "But he's still not married yet."

These days, my parents always compare my twin daughters to each other—which annoys me to no end. One of the many parenting books I've read specifically says, "Do not compare your twins." (Obviously, my mom didn't read that book.) When my mom watches them, she will observe that one of them runs faster than the other or one of them eats more than the other. That's just how she operates. But I don't want my kids to grow up feeling like they have to be in constant comparison with each other or anyone else. They just have to be themselves.

Competition can be healthy if it motivates you to do better, strive for greater goals, or try something new. But lifting yourself up by bringing others down? Comparing yourself or your kids to others because you feel there isn't enough opportunity or praise to go around? That's not a good tactic in parenting or in life. Ultimately, it will only lead you to unhappiness.

In the end, the only person you are really competing with is yourself. Ask yourself if you're proud of what you've done—did you do the best with the resources available to you? What did you learn? What will you do differently going forward? As long as you are growing as a person and moving in the right direction, you're on the right track.

JOY PRESCRIPTION

Break Free from Comparison

- *Avoid comparing other people's outside to your inside.* For example, if you're comparing yourself to someone from what you see on their social media, remember that you're comparing your daily life to their greatest hits. It's simply not a fair comparison.
- *Focus on your own triumphs.* Make a list of your accomplishments. Just because someone is farther along than you doesn't mean *you* haven't come a long way in *your* journey. Sometimes it's helpful to write it all down so you can see all the things you've accomplished and how far you've come.
- *Use the comparison as motivation.* If someone has something you want, take a look at what steps they've taken to get there. Instead of comparison, might there be potential for a learning experience? Many successful people are more than happy to share their wisdom and lessons learned.

CHAPTER 3

BLINDERS

The day before graduation from Cornell University, age nineteen

SEVERAL YEARS AGO, A FRIEND INVITED ME TO A KENTUCKY Derby party. I don't know anything about horses or horse racing, but I thought it was a good excuse to wear a cute outfit with a big hat. As we sat there with our mint juleps, watching the horses race, my friend turned to me and asked, "Do you know why that horse is wearing that thing on its head?"

I looked at the hood that covered most of the horse's face and figured that it was there because it matched the outfit of the jockey—in the same way that my hat matched my dress.

"It's for identification?" I guessed. "So that you can tell which horse goes with which jockey?"

"Not quite," my friend said.

Okay, I figured I should think about this more seriously. "It's for aerodynamic efficiency. It decreases the drag coefficient so the horse can run faster."

"Smarter answer, but no."

"Then what is it for?"

"Notice the parts of the hood that are around the eyes of the horse? They're called blinders. They're used to decrease the horse's peripheral vision so that it's only focused on the finish line. So that it doesn't lose a tenth of a second looking somewhere else."

The more I thought about it, the more I realized that this analogy of wearing blinders described the way I'd grown up. All my life, I'd had a metaphorical hood around my head that blocked out everything but the road in front of me that led to the finish line. No looking to the left or right, no distractions, and definitely no stopping. Does this sound familiar to you? I was so focused on the end result that everything else fell by the wayside. But unlike the horses, I found that every time I reached what I thought was the finish line, *it moved*. I felt like I could never catch up.

AFTER TAMS, THE NEXT FINISH LINE THAT I SET FOR MYSELF—OR rather, that my parents set for me—was graduating from Cornell University in two years. Why Cornell, you ask? It wasn't because I loved trudging through snow five months out of the year or walking over steep ravines to get to class. It was because Cornell was the best school that I got into that would take both years of credits from TAMS.

As long as I could remember, my dad had lived and died by the *U.S. News and World Report* Best Colleges rankings. That was his

Bible. He had the top twenty schools memorized. When it was time to apply for "real" college, he handed me the list and said, "Apply to top twenty." So I did, and I got into most of them. The only problem was that very few of them would accept all my credits from TAMS. The school I had really wanted to go to said it would take all my credits, but I could not graduate in under four years. "Why you go to TAMS if you still need to go to college for four more years?" my dad said. "Go to Cornell. Finish in two years. Save money and time." And that was the end of that discussion. Without ever visiting a single college campus, I signed the acceptance letter and mailed it with a check to Cornell University.

I was seventeen when I set foot on campus at Cornell as an incoming junior, not knowing a single person and definitely not adequately prepared for the winter. Having come from Texas, I didn't even own a proper coat. To get all my premed classes in and graduate in two years, I would have to take an average of eighteen credits per semester. And if I didn't want to take a gap year, which my dad said would be a waste of time, I would need to take the MCAT during my second semester while taking a full course load. I was on a one-way (high-speed) train to medical school, and there was no way I could get off.

My first semester, I took the most dreaded premed class—organic chemistry. My first test came back with a large red "56%" circled at the top. *Fifty-six percent.* The test had been difficult, but I hadn't thought I had failed. I turned the paper over and back again, hoping that the numbers would miraculously change, but they stayed the same. A deep sense of shame came over me. Maybe I didn't deserve to be here; maybe I was in over my head. How disappointed my parents would be when I failed out of Cornell.

To understand my reaction, you have to understand the Asian grading scale:

Average
Below average
Can't eat dinner
Don't come home
Find new family

My mind swarmed with thoughts. Maybe I wasn't that smart after all. Maybe before, I had just been a big fish in a small pond. This was Cornell, full of brilliant students from all over the country and the world. Who was I to think I could compete in the big leagues?

The only thing I could do was study even harder. Often I slept only three or four hours a night to squeeze in more studying. Accepting invitations to parties or hanging out with my classmates? Forget it. At first I thought about joining the Chinese Student Association, the figure skating club, or a sorority, but after failing that organic chemistry test, the thought of making friends didn't matter anymore. (As my dad liked to remind me, he wasn't paying $30,000 a year for me to make new friends.) After a while, people stopped asking me to go out for Korean barbecue or to karaoke night. What was the point? I was always studying. Once, I remember being jolted awake by someone tapping me on the shoulder and saying, "The library is closing; you need to go home." I peeled my slobber-smeared face off my biochemistry textbook. Time to change locations, grab a cup of coffee, and keep studying.

I don't have many regrets in life, but one of them is that I didn't take the time to enjoy my college experience. The Cornell campus had so much natural beauty, the student body was so diverse, and the course offerings were so abundant, but I didn't take advantage of any of that. There were virtually no fun classes for me, no extracurriculars, no studying abroad. When I ventured to ask my dad whether I could study abroad, he said, "What can you learn in another country that you can't learn here?" *A lot, actually.* But I didn't argue with him. "Yes, Baba, you're right. Sorry I brought it up. I wasn't thinking."

What are your greatest memories of college? Taking a certain class or extracurricular? Making lifelong friends? Celebrating your graduation day? Mine were none of those. The greatest memory I have is the day I found out I'd been accepted into my number-one choice for medical school. I treated college as a necessary stepping stone on my journey to becoming a doctor rather than treating it like the unique experience it was. For two years, I ran on caffeine, adrenaline, and fear. The fear of failure. The fear of disappointing my parents. The fear that the people around me would figure out that I wasn't actually that smart. And if I didn't have smart, I didn't have anything. That's all I'd ever had.

I was that racehorse with blinders on, speeding toward the finish line. I couldn't look at anything else, focus on anything except that finish line. Along the way, I missed out on crucial experiences like forming deep friendships, making college memories, and enjoying the learning process. Nothing mattered except fulfilling my parents' expectations of me, which somehow had also become my expectations of myself, even if I didn't completely understand them. All I knew was that when I finished college, I would be one step closer to getting those two illustrious letters after my name, and then maybe—just maybe—my parents would be proud of me.

But at the end of those two years, my dad didn't even meet me at the finish line—he didn't come to my graduation ceremony. Cornell University, located in Ithaca, New York, is notoriously difficult to get to. From Dallas, my parents would have had to fly into New York City or another major East Coast city, then take another flight to a local airport, and then rent a car or take a bus to get to campus. There would also have been the cost of staying at a hotel, with the price inflated by the thousands of parents coming in for graduation. It would be too much trouble and cost too much money—the two excuses that will get you out of doing just about anything in my family.

On the telephone, my dad told me that my mom would be the only one attending my graduation: "Josh and I will stay home."

Trying to hold back tears, I said, "I'm really disappointed that you won't be there." It was the first time that I had ever said something like this to my dad, conveying the hurt that I felt on the inside.

"For what?" my dad asked. "Spend thousands of dollars and come there to see you walk across the stage and accept a piece of paper? Tell me this. If I come or don't come, do you still graduate? Are you still going to medical school? Focus on what's important. Don't be stupid."

Again, my feeling of disappointment turned into guilt. *Dad is right*, I thought. It *was* just a piece of paper. (Never mind one that I'd worked my ass off for.) I tried to focus on everything I had achieved—that I had managed to graduate in two years (with honors) and been accepted to medical school without needing to take a gap year. I tried to feel happy, grateful, and optimistic. But all I felt was the extreme mental and physical exhaustion that came from running this race.

I should have stopped and taken the time to enjoy this significant moment in my life. When other people reach a milestone like this, they celebrate with their loved ones, with a party or a dinner or some kind of special event. But I did nothing. My mom arrived for graduation. She stayed in my dorm with me to save money on renting a hotel room, sleeping in my bed while I slept on the floor. Then she sat in the sun (every Asian mom's worst nightmare) for a few hours to watch me walk across the stage and accept a piece of paper. Then we packed up my stuff and went back to Dallas, where medical school awaited me. I thought I had made it to the finish line, but the finish line had moved.

⌒

IF YOU'RE SENSING A PATTERN TO MY LIFE SO FAR, YOU'D PROBABLY guess that medical school would be like my previous experiences—lots of studying, worrying about achievement, and feeling like an imposter. Sure, there was some of that. But as it turned out, medical school was the time of my life.

Now you're probably thinking, *Wow, she must be a really big dork if she had the time of her life in medical school.* But you have to understand that this was the first time I'd be going to the same school for all four years. There was no way for me to graduate early from med school, even if I wanted (or my dad wanted me) to. This was the first time I could make new friends and enjoy learning for the sake of it. On top of that, rather than taking a class like organic chemistry and wondering when I would ever use this information, I was learning about the human body, meeting people from all walks of life, and discovering things that changed my perception of the world and my place in it.

As I sat in freshman orientation with about two hundred other medical students, I felt a sense of belonging that I had never felt before. *I belong here,* I thought. *I deserve to be here. I am a sponge—I am ready to learn. And I'm also ready to have a little fun.*

The first semester in med school, you're assigned "tankmates" to dissect a cadaver in Gross Anatomy, which means that you spend hours upon hours with the same people. My tankmates were Lisa and Michelle. Like me, Lisa was Chinese American—she had attended UC Berkeley and was obsessed with Harry Potter and baking. Michelle, also from Dallas, had gone to Rice University and loved sports, especially baseball. I was the girl coming from New

York who loved fashion and skincare. I had never read a single Harry Potter book or been to a baseball game. Although we had very different interests, the three of us became immediate best friends. We bonded over the fact that we were all single, had brothers but not sisters, and were learning the foundations of medicine side by side. One of our classmates dubbed us "the Happy Triad"—a play on the term "unhappy triad," which refers to a blown knee—and the three of us were inseparable for the next four years.

About a month in, the gross anatomy dissection came to the urinary and reproductive systems. "Make sure you study the anatomy of a neighboring cadaver that is the opposite sex of your own cadaver," the professor instructed us. The next day, when Lisa, Michelle, and I started to take a look at our cadaver's genitals, we discovered something stuck in the vaginal canal.

"What is that?" Lisa asked.

"Is that a...oh my gosh, I think that's a..." Michelle stuttered.

"Let me see; here, give it to me," I said, grabbing it with my forceps.

It was a penis. A penis that had been severed from our neighboring cadaver and put inside the vagina of our cadaver.

The three of us shrieked. It turned out that one of our classmates— the class clown—had pulled this little stunt as a practical joke. Soon our shrieks turned into laughter. But the teaching assistants weren't laughing.

The next day we were called into the dean's office. I was thinking, *Oh my gosh. If I get kicked out of med school after everything I've done to get here over a penis prank...*

After being lectured about the sanctity of medicine and the sacrifice of people who had donated their bodies to science, we ended up being assigned to a class about professionalism and ordered to perform some community service. Our classmate who had played the prank took the fall and told the dean it was all his fault and we had nothing to do with it. (He ended up going on to become a well-respected pediatrician and faculty member at one of the best medical schools in the world, where his practical jokes are a little less crude.)

The first two years of medical school, everyone went to the same classes, so the three of us were almost always together. But in our third year, the Happy Triad was broken up as we split up for clinical rotations. After two years of class and lab work, we were finally going to get some hands-on experience with real patients.

My first rotation was psychiatry, where I saw things beyond my wildest imagination. On my first day, I waltzed into the psychiatric unit with my stethoscope draped casually around my neck as I'd seen the attending doctors do around the hospital.

"Take your stethoscope off," my senior resident instructed. "You don't want a patient to try to strangle you with it."

In the psychiatric ER, there was a centralized holding room where the patients, with the exception of those in solitary confinement, were placed. We med students were responsible for helping the residents take a history and physical exam and then going over the plan with the attending physicians. Sometimes we sat behind a two-way mirror to observe the patients.

One day the police brought in a homeless woman with schizophrenia who became agitated in the holding room. She appeared to be arguing with someone, and then all of a sudden, she took off her pants, squatted, and defecated on the floor. Then she scooped up her feces and started throwing it at the door while screaming, "Get away from me!"

What part of med school was this? There was no way anything I had learned in class or from a textbook could have prepared me. I felt helpless because I didn't know what to do. The attending said, "Give her some vitamin H," and shortly after, two guards held her down and a nurse jabbed her arm with haloperidol, an antipsychotic, while she struggled and shouted profanities.

When I opened her chart, there were multiple pages of notes describing similar scenarios where the police had found her wandering around by the highway or a concerned citizen had seen her outside with no shoes on when it was 105 degrees. She had ended up in the psychiatric ER many times, and each time she'd been discharged with an appointment to see a psychiatrist and a prescription for medication. But none of it seemed to be doing any good.

I asked my resident, "What are we going to do for her this time to make her better? Seems like she's been here several times but keeps coming back."

He looked at me and said, "All we can do is try our best."

Working in a public (safety-net) hospital, I saw all kinds of things, from people who had been shot and stabbed to people who were experiencing all kinds of unimaginable hardship, illness, and violence. I'd never really thought of myself as having grown up sheltered until I started my clinical rotations.

During my surgery rotation, a severely burned patient was airlifted from a nearby state because our hospital was a world-class burn center. A victim of domestic abuse, she'd told her husband that she was planning to leave him. That night, in their bedroom, while their toddler slept next door, he'd doused her with lighter fluid and set her on fire. I'll never forget the smell of burned flesh when she came into the operating room, intubated and with her eyes swollen shut. We learned in lecture that a score was used to calculate your risk of death with burn injuries—you add the patient's age to the percentage of body surface area burned. When a patient scores above 100, the chance that they will survive is basically 0 percent.

This patient was twenty-eight years old with 60 percent of her body burned. She was in the hospital for four months and had three dozen surgeries to graft skin from the unburned parts of her body to the burned parts. Even after I finished my surgery rotation, I continued to swing by to visit her as she recovered. As she was getting close to being transferred to another hospital, she confided in me that she was grateful for what had happened because she knew she was going to make it, and at least now her husband was in jail so she could get away from him. I couldn't believe that someone who had just been through what she had was expressing gratitude. I hugged her, wished her well, and walked out of her room forever changed by the realization that our *interpretation* of what happened to us is much more powerful than what *actually* happened to us.

Still, I was shaken by the amount of pain I saw humans inflict on other humans. *How can one person do this to another?* I asked myself. Of course I had seen terrible things before on the news—the numerous ways in which people could hurt one another—but it was abstract, whereas in the hospital, everything became more real. During my third-year rotations, I witnessed the dark underbelly of human nature that most people never get to see up close, and it toughened me a bit. There is a common bond among health-care workers because you see the aftermath of people intentionally hurting one another or themselves, patients sick with terminal illnesses, and innocent children who you know won't make it to the next grade in school. These experiences harden us because we have to be able to emotionally detach from them or we wouldn't be able to do our jobs. After a while, because you're so used to suppressing your feelings, you forget how to be attuned to your emotions and how to connect with other people. For me, being good at suppressing my feelings was a double-edged sword because I functioned well in the hospital, but outside work, I found myself detached and struggled to connect with my emotions.

The first person I ever sutured up was drunk and high on cocaine—he had crashed his car into a wall and was bleeding profusely from his scalp.

"You know how to suture?" my resident asked me.

"Yeah, we practiced in lab the other day," I replied.

"Here's some suture—go close up his head."

See one, do one, teach one was the motto of med school.

That same night, another level 1 trauma came in a little after 3 a.m. A man had tried to kill himself by shooting his gun directly upward into his chin. But that doesn't kill you—it just blows off the front of your face. I wondered what had happened that had made him want to take his own life. We took him to the operating room, where we secured his airway so that the surgeons could assess the extent of his injuries. I got to see an awake fiber-optic intubation for the first time, which fascinated me. I wondered if, when he woke up from surgery, he'd feel that he'd been given a second chance at life or that he'd been robbed of his death.

As I rotated through the different specialties of medicine, I was exposed to just how precarious the line between life and death was. On my internal medicine rotation, I had a patient in the ICU who had pneumonia and was on a ventilator. Every day we did a sponta-neous breathing trial to see if he was ready to breathe on his own, and every day he failed. He loved all things Star Trek and collecting Mr. Potato Heads—he was surrounded by several that his family had brought in to comfort him. Since he was intubated and couldn't talk, he had a pen and clipboard that he would scribble on to com-municate with us.

Two weeks into his ICU stay, as I was rounding, I asked him if he felt strong enough to pass his breathing trial that day. He wrote, "No. Enough. I am ready to go." Scientifically speaking, his chronic obstructive pulmonary disease (COPD) was severe, and his pneu-monia had made his lungs too weak for him to be extubated. Emo-tionally, he had come to terms with the fact that his body was failing him and that his time had come.

We had a meeting with his family, and the doctors presented the scenario—they could perform a tracheostomy (a hole in his neck making a direct connection to his windpipe), and he would likely be dependent on a machine to help him breathe, or they could withdraw care, allowing nature to take its course. The family decided to withdraw care. "It's what Dad wants," his daughter said. "He doesn't want to be connected to a machine for the rest of his life."

The next day I stood with his family as they gathered at his bedside. We made sure that he was comfortable, and he even scribbled some jokes on his clipboard like "The time has come." The respiratory therapist came in and turned off the ventilator, and an eerie silence filled the room—no more whooshing sounds as the ventilator gave him a breath every six seconds. At first he smiled as his family held his hands. After several minutes, he started flickering his eyelids and the EKG started to look irregular. After several more minutes, his eyes shut and his heart rate flatlined. The nurse pressed the silence button on the monitor, waited a minute, and then shut off the monitor altogether. "He's in a better place now," she said to the family. I left the room to give the family privacy and went to the doctor's station to write the official death note. He was the first patient whom I'd really gotten to know well who had died, and I was devastated.

As I was typing, trying to stay professional and keep it together, his wife approached me.

"Tiffany, I just want to thank you for everything you did," she said. "He enjoyed seeing you every day. He wanted you to have this."

Confused, I looked up to see her holding one of his Mr. Potato Heads—his favorite one, known as "Darth Tater." I reached out, took Darth Tater in my hand, and promptly burst into tears in front of her and everyone else in the ICU. I quickly thanked her and ran to the bathroom, where I sat on the floor and cried for the next fifteen minutes.

Just as I experienced the sorrows of death, I was reminded of the miracle of life. During my rotation in obstetrics and gynecology, I got to deliver several babies. At the time, our hospital had one of the busiest labor and delivery (L&D) units in the world, averaging around seventeen thousand deliveries a year. There were so many laboring women that sometimes they would overflow into the hallway and labor there, separated by thin curtains that hung on sliding racks from the ceiling.

The first time I helped deliver a baby, I had been on the rotation for one week and had no idea what I was doing. The junior resident tossed me a white baby blanket printed with pastel footprints and told me, "Gown up. And whatever you do, do *not* drop the baby. They're slippery."

I could barely catch a ball—how was I going to catch a baby? My general reaction when balls were thrown at me was to duck, not catch. What would happen if I dropped the baby? What if I hurt the baby? Would I fail this rotation?

All my doubts melted away when I caught that baby in the blanket and held it while the father cut the umbilical cord, and then I placed the baby on the mother's chest for skin-to-skin contact. I was standing there teary-eyed and smiling at the family when my resident said, "Sun, get back down here—we still need to deliver the placenta." *Oh, right, the placenta.* Sure, I had read about the placenta and looked at drawings of it in my *Netter Atlas of Human Anatomy*, studying the veins and arteries that ran together to supply the growing fetus. But I had never seen a placenta in real life before. As I gently pulled the end of the umbilical cord where we had clamped, the placenta came bursting out. It was dark purple, slippery, and bigger than I would have imagined.

"Can I keep it?" the woman asked.

"Huh?" I said, thinking she was talking about the baby. *Of course you can keep it; it's yours.*

Luckily my resident knew what she meant and replied, "I'm sorry, ma'am, it is our hospital's policy not to allow patients to keep the placenta." (This was before the Kardashians made it trendy to freeze-dry your placenta into pills to ingest postpartum.)

But perhaps one of the most memorable experiences I had in med school—one that really opened my eyes to reality—happened not inside the hospital but just outside it.

One day, when I was walking out of the hospital to go home, a woman came up to me. I thought she was going to ask me for directions, but instead she held out a booklet of stamps.

"You wanna buy this?" she asked. "I'll sell it to you for cash. It's a hundred, but I'll give it to you for fifty."

I was confused at first. I had never seen food stamps before and didn't understand her question. My first instinct was that she was selling tickets to some sort of sporting event. Then it hit me that she was trying to sell her food stamps for half their value for cash. I dug into my backpack and took out a five-dollar bill and some change and handed it to her, mumbling, "Sorry, this is all I have." On the way home, I wondered what exactly she needed the cash for and if she had kids at home who were hungry and needed her. And that made my heart hurt in a way it never had before.

I thought about how, as poor as my family was while I was growing up, we'd never had it as bad as this woman and the kids she probably had at home. I never worried about where my next meal would come from or not having a place to sleep. All of a sudden, I felt guilty that I'd complained about my parents being so hard on me, always wanting me to study harder and be better. *I should be more grateful*, I thought. *I had it pretty good.*

The blinders were starting to come off, in more ways than one. In my personal life, I had a fantastic group of friends. In school, I was being exposed to new experiences and taking the time to look around me at the world beyond my books. While I was witnessing the capacity of people to do both good and bad to one another, I was also inspired. I was surrounded by brilliant classmates with diverse interests and backgrounds. I could see a direct line from my dream as a little girl of being a doctor and helping people to what I was doing now. Someday all my hard work would be worth it.

During my fourth year in med school, I had to decide which specialty to apply to. Choosing a medical specialty is probably the most important decision you can make as a medical student—it's like choosing whom you're going to marry. It determines what you're going to do for the rest of your life.

One of my favorite rotations was surgery. I loved being in the operating room—the sterile environment, the rules that everyone had to follow, the careful dance that occurred with each operation. Everyone had a role and worked toward a common goal, and I loved the orderliness of it all. I also enjoyed internal medicine—taking a history and physical, ordering tests, trying to figure out what was wrong with the patient—but it all happened too slowly for me. I hated going home without definitive answers and would often log in to the computer on my days off to see what test results had come in while I was out. Both Lisa and Michelle were set on pediatrics, so I considered that as well until I did my pediatrics rotation. I liked children, but I didn't think I could handle sick children (and their parents). It was too difficult for me emotionally to work with children with chronic diseases that I knew could be managed but not cured. I tried to like dermatology because I love skincare, but medical dermatology was not appealing to me, and I just couldn't deal with the different rashes people had—they all made me feel itchy.

Anesthesiology was the perfect specialty for me. I liked that I was able to take the physiology and pharmacology I learned in the classroom and apply it to taking care of a patient during surgery. The intensity and precision of anesthesiology also appealed to my personality. The control freak in me loved being in control of everything—blood pressure too low? *No problem, I'll fix it.* The anatomy is complex and the patient is losing a lot of blood? *No problem, I'll fix it.* I liked being able to use my knowledge and skills to *do something* for the patient. Many times on other rotations, I wanted to *do more* but couldn't. I also loved the *immediate* gratification of anesthesiology, especially since my whole life, I had been living for *delayed* gratification. There is a certain amount of closure that comes with practicing anesthesiology, and it appealed to me greatly.

Most of all, anesthesiology requires a responsible person, and responsibility is my jam. If I had my own perfume, I'd call it *Responsibility* by Tiffany Moon. What does that smell like, you ask? It smells like always paying your bills on time, being everyone's "in case of emergency" contact, and remembering to bring a fresh stool sample to the dog's vet appointment. Fine, I may not be the life of the party, but you can definitely count on me to get things done—and done well.

On Match Day, which is arguably *the* most important day of med school, you find out where you are going to be spending the next three to seven years of your life as a resident physician. My entire class gathered in the atrium of the medical school, and at 10 a.m. sharp, we opened our mailboxes, where a single envelope and piece of paper would declare our fate. I carefully tore open my envelope and stared at the paper inside—Internal Medicine, Dallas Presbyterian Hospital; Anesthesiology, UC San Francisco. I had done it! I had matched at my number-one programs. When I looked up from the paper, I saw Michelle first and then Lisa, both of whom were smiling from ear to ear. I knew it—they had both matched into their first-choice programs as well. We had done it. The Happy Triad was three for three!

I was in the homestretch. But even though I was still racing toward that finish line, the circumstances had changed. Now I was taking the time to look at my surroundings. To learn from something other than what was in the classroom and my books. To apply what I had learned to real life and to enjoy the journey along the way.

It's great to have goals. Goals motivate you, get you up in the morning, and make you put in that extra ounce of effort. But when the end point is all that you focus on, you can lose sight of other things that are important. You might ignore the little things that make up the fabric of your life, like the people you interact with every day. Most of all, you might not listen to the part of you that's telling you that you need to rest, to take some time for yourself, or to make a change.

Have you ever reached a goal in your life and felt disappointed because it wasn't everything you thought it was going to be? Maybe the finish line moved or the goal changed. Maybe you realized that you missed out on a lot along the way, and perhaps those sacrifices weren't worth it. The good news is that once you're aware, you can choose how you run your next race.

I did not take off my blinders overnight, and you won't be able to either—the experience would be too jarring. Opening your eyes to the full horizon of life is a gradual process, and in some ways, committing to taking off the blinders can be harder than keeping your head down and doing what you've always done. But if you want to change your attitude toward life, it's worth it. Because only when we strip away the expectations that others have set for us can we finally see what we want for ourselves.

JOY PRESCRIPTION

Focus on the Journey, Not the Destination

- *Ask why you set a particular goal for yourself.* Was it something you truly wanted, or was it a goal based on the expectations or priorities of others? The next time you set a goal, how can you make it your own?
- *Don't be afraid of taking detours.* The path to your destination may not be a straight line. There may be side paths, and you might make mistakes along the way, but these are learning experiences that can be just as valuable as reaching the goal itself.
- *Enjoy the process.* When you take the time to appreciate the scenery and experiences along the way to your destination, chances are you will feel happier, more fulfilled, and more present throughout the process. And you might just find new opportunities that you would have missed if you had focused only on the finish line.

CHAPTER 4

GOOD ON PAPER

Getting married in Hawaii

A S A FACULTY MEMBER AT A TEACHING HOSPITAL, I MENTOR quite a few medical students and residents. They come to me for all sorts of advice, from choosing a medical specialty to navigating their romantic relationships. Over and over again, I'm asked for advice on medicine, life, and love. Now, I'm no relationship expert, but I'd like to think that I have some wisdom when it comes to matters of the heart.

Once, one of my residents sought my help to choose a ring to propose to his girlfriend. Between cases in the operating room, we assessed the merits of a classic diamond shape like round or princess versus a more contemporary shape like marquise or pear. A few months later, he texted me a picture of him and his girlfriend on vacation together with her wearing the beautiful ring he'd picked out and a caption that said, "Dr. Moon—she said *yes!*"

Another resident pulled me aside at the end of the day and said, "Dr. Moon, can I ask you about something personal?"

"Of course," I replied.

"I really love my boyfriend, but he got laid off from his job over six months ago and still hasn't found a new job. He says he's looking, but when I get home, he's usually playing video games online."

"Have you spoken to him about this?"

"No, he just gets so defensive every time I bring it up."

"Maybe he realized he doesn't love that career path and wants to pivot in a new direction but feels scared or doesn't know how to tell you. I really think you should try to have a chat with him in a nonconfrontational, 'I just want to understand what's going through your mind' kind of way."

"But he keeps avoiding me."

"Change the Wi-Fi password," I said, deadpan. "That'll get his attention real quick."

These days, I'm constantly amazed at the plethora of different online dating options out there. My mentees tell me that they're busy swiping left or right and answering esoteric question prompts to see if their answers might spark someone's interest enough to match with them. Sometimes they'll let me peek over their shoulder while they navigate through these dating apps, and it's always overwhelming to me. There are so many options and so many questions that are somehow supposed to determine your compatibility with a potential mate. What's your most irrational fear? If you could have one super-power, which would you choose and why? What's the weirdest thing you've done? Then you need to upload a few photos—one of you traveling so you seem worldly, one of you with friends so you seem social, one of you showing off your physique but in a non-showing-off kind of way (or else you'll be labeled a thirst trap), and one more of you working or doing something studious so they know you're serious and not just all fun and games. Hot damn, just looking at all the questions and doing all that swiping gave me a headache.

As I chat with these young people, I think, *If dating had worked this way back when I was still single, I would never have met my husband.* There would have been no swiping on him because he wouldn't even have shown up in my search results.

When people ask, "How did you meet your husband?" I would love to say, "We went to school together" or "We met at church," but that's simply not the truth. I met Daniel the good old-fashioned way—at a bar. Okay, fine, it wasn't just a bar. Actually, it was a full-on nightclub—complete with a DJ playing the latest hip-hop songs, scantily clad "bottle girls," and VIP tables partitioned off with velvet ropes. Classy, I know. We met on a random Thursday night the month before I graduated from medical school. I was done with all my coursework and had just matched into my number-one residency program, so I was in full-on senioritis mode. A group of us went out to celebrate and joked to one another, "Hey, are you ready for people to start calling you 'Doctor'?" What I was not ready for was a guy who bumped into me on the dance floor and spilled my drink. I looked at him in disbelief.

"I'm so sorry," he said. "Let's go to the bar and I'll buy you another drink."

I followed him to the bar, and we got to talking for a bit. Then he said, "What was your name again? Tiffany? Tiffany, I'd like you to meet my friend Daniel." And there Daniel was, standing across from me. (No, the guy who spilled my drink wasn't my future husband—that would have been too cute—but that guy did lead me to Daniel, and to this day, I swear that Daniel sent him on purpose to spill my drink.)

As I sipped my new cocktail, Daniel asked me what my friends and I were celebrating, and I told him that in a month, we would all be graduating from medical school. You know how when you meet a stranger, and they mention that they go to a certain school, and you're like "Oh do you know so-and-so?" and of course they never do because that school is full of thousands of people, and what are the chances? Well, after I told Daniel that I was in medical school, he asked if I knew so-and-so, and in fact I had worked with that specific so-and-so in the operating room several times because he was an anesthesiology resident. Apparently they were best friends. I mean, what were the odds? That shared connection made me feel a bit better since I usually wasn't keen on chatting with random guys I met in clubs.

At the end of the night, Daniel asked for my number, and I happily gave it to him—the real one, not the fake number I usually gave out. I warned him, though—"If I don't pick up, it's because in two days, I'm leaving for a monthlong trip to Australia with my friend" and pointed to Michelle, who nodded in agreement and smirked at me. I thought about Daniel a bit while I was traveling, but honestly, Michelle and I were so busy hiking, scuba diving in the Great Barrier Reef, and making new friends that I didn't think about home much while we were in Australia.

When I returned, Daniel texted me, asking how my trip was. We chatted on the phone a few times before he asked if I wanted to grab dinner sometime.

"I don't know," I said. "I just got out of a bad relationship, and I'm just not ready for anything serious right now."

There was a pause. "I asked if you wanted to go out for dinner sometime; I didn't ask if you wanted to marry me," he said jokingly. (Spoiler alert: he did eventually ask me to marry him but not for a few more years.)

"Ohhh, right, dinner," I replied bashfully. "Well, I do eat every day, so I guess that would work for me. How's next Thursday night?"

When Thursday rolled around, I started panicking and wondering what I had gotten myself into. The trouble was, several weeks had passed since Daniel and I had first met, and at the time, I'd been tipsy and in a dark nightclub. I couldn't really remember what he looked like.

I called Michelle. "Hey, you know that guy we met in the club right before we left for Australia? I'm going out to dinner with him tonight. You think that's okay, right?"

"Yeah, didn't you say his best friend is that anesthesia resident you know?" she said.

I nodded. "He was cute, right?"

"Yes, he was cute. Now, go have fun!"

With Michelle's blessing, I started looking forward to our date. I had no real expectations going in, and so I felt free to just enjoy myself. In my previous dating life, I had been a serial monogamist. I'd met every one of my past boyfriends through school. I'd never dated multiple guys at the same time, I'd never had a one-night stand, I'd never had a wild streak. So I thought, *Let's try something new: Why don't I just have fun?* No making the guy jump through hoops or playing games. No interrogation about where he'd gone to school, his SAT scores, and his future life goals. No waiting for the third date before kissing. If I wanted to kiss this guy at the end of our first date, I would do it. (This was my idea of sexual liberation.)

I put on my favorite black-and-white halter dress from bebe that showed off a little cleavage but wasn't too tight or skimpy. Daniel came to my apartment to pick me up. I wasn't expecting anything fancy, but he insisted that we go to Nobu. I was impressed by this choice because earlier on the phone, he had asked what my favorite food was, and I'd said sushi. "Great, I love sushi too. My favorite place is Nobu—have you been there before?" he'd asked. Ummm, no. I had not been to Nobu. I had almost six figures of student-loan debt and was in no position to afford twenty-four-dollar tuna sashimi. My favorite sushi spot was a hole in the wall near the med school that had two-for-one rolls on Tuesday nights.

Daniel and I hit it off immediately. We had a similar sense of humor (dry and a little sarcastic) and shared interests, and the conversation flowed easily. We both loved traveling and traded stories of where we'd been and where we'd like to go in the future. I told him that my dream was to travel to Paris, walk along the Champs-Élysées, visit the flagship Hermès store, and see the Eiffel Tower at night when it was twinkling. He told me he'd never been to China and asked if I would go with him and show him the city where I'd grown up. He told me that he loved to try new recipes in the kitchen and asked if I liked to cook. I hesitated briefly, hearing my mom's voice in the back of my head: "You need to learn to cook, or no man will want to marry you."

"No, I don't like cooking," I answered, "but I could come up with some mean wine pairings—a sparkling brut rosé to start, then a dry white like a sauvignon blanc, and then either a pinot noir or a cabernet sauvignon, depending on the main course."

He smiled and said, "Perfect—so we can play chef and sommelier? Your place or mine?" There was just an immediate spark and chemistry that I had never felt before.

Then came the bombshell.

"I should tell you something," Daniel said. "I'm divorced."

"Okay," I said.

"And I have two kids."

Oh well, there goes that, I thought. *Thanks for dinner.*

I really thought that would be our first and last date, but against my better judgment, I continued to see Daniel. Have you ever met someone who makes you feel alive, free, and, most of all, happy? That was how he made me feel. He brought out a side of me that I didn't know existed. We were just having so much fun. I had planned to stay in Dallas to do my internal medicine internship for a year before starting my anesthesiology residency in San Francisco. I figured nothing serious could happen in that time, so why not just go with the flow?

I was also convinced that anything with Daniel couldn't possibly last because of how fundamentally different we were. In addition to being divorced with two kids, he was eleven years older and wasn't a doctor. (For some reason, I'd always thought I would marry another doctor.) Oh, and he was Korean. Now, you might be thinking, Chinese and Korean…those are kind of similar, right? They both eat lots of rice, study a ton, and have strict parents. Maybe, but there are a lot of differences too. However, we couldn't even start to discuss those differences because my parents could not see beyond his being Korean and previously married with kids.

A few months into our relationship, I decided to test the waters and tell my mom about him. My mom's ideal dating timeline is as follows:

Age 1–22: No dating; you need to study!

Age 23–25: You know Auntie Chen? She have a son, very smart, graduate from Yale.

Age 25+: Why you not married yet? I want to have grandson.

One day I told her with some hesitation that I was kind of seeing someone.

"Oh? You have a new boyfriend? You meet him in hospital?" she asked (one doctor in the family is good, but two is better).

"No, Mom, not in the hospital. His name is Daniel. He's a lawyer and an entrepreneur." My mom smiled, so I kept going. "He's very kind, funny, and thoughtful. He likes to cook for me." She was still smiling but stayed silent. "He's a little bit older than me. He's Korean, and he was married before, and he's got two kids, four-year-old twins."

My mom's smile turned into a frown. "Daddy not going to like this."

No shit, that's why I'm telling you first. I knew that all these things looked bad. They looked bad on paper, and they would look bad to my parents' church friends. But what was I supposed to do? Sometimes you can't help whom you fall in love with.

I had been in a few relationships before, and yes, I had cared for my previous boyfriends, but I had never felt the head-over-heels sort of love that I felt with Daniel. *Maybe this was lust? Wasn't that one of the seven deadly sins? Was this going to crash and burn?* I thought. *Oh my god, is this it? Is this what people write songs about and what those romantic movies are about?* I used to roll my eyes when I heard expressions like "He swept me off my feet," and now *I* was the one telling all my friends he'd swept me off my feet. Falling in love with Daniel was very sudden and happened when I was least expecting it. I was definitely not out looking for love that Thursday night at the club with my medical school friends. If you had told me that I'd meet my future husband that night, I would have laughed. But this was becoming serious quickly. It felt like fate had brought us together and he was my soulmate. I could not imagine ever being without him.

Halfway through my intern year, when things were getting pretty serious, I started contemplating staying in Dallas instead of moving to San Francisco for my anesthesia residency. When I told Michelle, she said, "Absolutely not! As long as I've known you, you've wanted to move to San Francisco. You told me the day you matched at UCSF was one of the happiest days of your life. You're not going to give that up for some man. Even if you think that he's *the one*."

I thought about what she'd said and discussed it with Daniel. I felt torn—as if I had to choose either my career or my personal life. It just seemed to me that a three-year long-distance relationship between San Francisco and Dallas was destined to fail. In the end, I decided I needed to follow through on my original plan and move to SF. When I told Daniel, he said something that really hit me: "What's three years apart when we have the whole rest of our lives together?"

IN THOSE EARLY YEARS, DANIEL AND I WERE TESTED BY OUR PARents, our growing careers, and our efforts to maintain a relationship with more than three thousand miles between us.

In some ways, long distance was good for both of us. I was a resident working sixty to eighty hours a week. I lived, ate, and breathed anesthesia. If there was an emergency case that came in the evening, I would volunteer to take it. It wasn't as if I had anyone at home waiting for me. Often it would be a good learning case, and anesthesia is one of those specialties that you won't learn by reading a book.

Daniel was busy too. He was growing his business in real estate development and constantly traveling. In addition, he spent every other week with his kids. On the weekends that he wasn't with them, we made seeing each other a priority. Once, I was on call over the weekend and told him it was probably best to skip and see each other in two weeks, but he insisted on coming to San Francisco. As luck would have it, I got called in to do a liver transplant and was gone for twelve hours, during which he walked around Union Square and then stocked my fridge with groceries and did my laundry. When I got home, I was so exhausted that I showered and went to bed. When the alarm went off, it was Sunday afternoon and time for me to take him to the airport so he could go back to Dallas. We treasured our time together, and as they say, distance made our hearts grow fonder.

However, the relationship could also be very lonely. After a long day at the hospital, I desperately wanted to go home and be with someone I could talk to in person. Daniel and I talked on the phone often, but it wasn't the same. (I've never enjoyed talking on the phone—when people say they've been on the phone for hours with their friend, I think, *Why would you do that?*) It began to feel like we were leading separate lives that occasionally crossed.

Then there was the matter of introducing him to my parents.

My parents had met and approved of my previous two boyfriends. Both of them had gone to prestigious schools, were in medicine, and came from Chinese families who spoke Chinese and understood Chinese culture. Boyfriend #1 and I had been in medical school together. He was very nice, but we had very little in common except that we were both studying to be doctors. He liked playing tennis and video games and rarely wanted to go out, whereas I had no interest in tennis or video games and wanted to go out and try new things. There was nothing wrong with him—we were just incompatible, and after two years, we went our separate ways.

Boyfriend #2 was a few years older and already a doctor. He was tall, had more diverse interests, and loved to travel. But he suffered from classic spoiled-first-son-of-an-Asian-mom syndrome. When his mom visited, she would bring him Tupperware containers filled with food and instruct me on how to heat them up for him. She asked me if I cooked for him and did his laundry. *Hell, no.* We were on-again, off-again for almost two years, and whenever we were off, my friends would tell me not to get back together with him (isn't it funny how your friends always know?). I just wanted it to work because he was good on paper, and when times were good, they were good. The only problem was that they were good only about half the time. But I stayed because it was the path of least resistance.

What I learned from those two relationships, besides the fact that I did not want to cook or clean for someone like I was their mom, was that good on paper does not always mean good in real life. Sure, on paper those two guys should have been perfect for me. We came from the same cultural background, spoke the same language, and were in the same profession. But when it came down to what really mattered, they were not right for me.

You might have had a similar experience in a relationship in which the other person checked off all the boxes on your list about profession and family background and where they went to school. But are you able to check off the other boxes—about their beliefs, values, and future goals? Are you with someone because it's easy to stay, or are you with someone whom you can't imagine being without?

I was beginning to think more and more that Daniel was *the one*, and I didn't want to hide it anymore—especially from my parents. My first year in SF, I came home for Christmas and stayed at my parents' house. I didn't have my car with me, so I asked Daniel to come pick me up so we could go look at Christmas lights.

"Should he come inside and meet you and Dad?" I suggested to my mom.

She shook her head. "I don't think that's a good idea."

So I had to sneak out of my parents' house as if I were a teenager secretly meeting my boyfriend. But I wasn't a teenager. I was twenty-four years old—*I was a doctor*—and I was still afraid to bring my boyfriend home to my family.

A few months later, on another trip home, I told my dad that I needed to talk to him about something.

"Ummm, Dad, I've been seeing someone—"

I guess my mom had already prepped him because I barely had the chance to speak before he interrupted me: "You are a pretty and smart girl. You are a doctor. And you cannot find somebody better than that? Is that how I've raised you?"

I remained silent. However, I wasn't silent out of shame or guilt this time. I was livid. This wasn't like the time I'd asked my dad if I could take a semester to study abroad and he'd shot down the idea. Or when I'd suggested taking a gap year between college and medical school and he'd called me lazy. This time, I was asking my dad to give me the benefit of the doubt. He had raised me to have good judgment and to make good decisions. And now I needed him to trust me when I told him that Daniel was the man I wanted to be with. He had to accept that.

"Respectfully," I said to him, "I've done everything you've wanted me to. I went to Cornell and finished in two years. I went to med school and graduated at the top of my class. I got into the best anesthesiology residency in the country. I dated two guys that you approved of. They didn't make me happy. I didn't love them. I love Daniel."

"What do you know about love?" my dad said. "What you're feeling right now, it's not going to last. And you know those two kids? They'll never see you as their mom."

"Of course they won't," I retorted. "I'm *not* their mom."

"It's going to be difficult for you. Korean men cheat a lot." *I mean, how many K-dramas had he been watching?*

"I'm sorry you feel that way," I finally said. "I'm an adult—I'm almost twenty-five years old—and you have to trust that I can make decisions for myself."

My dad threw up his hands. "Do whatever you want. It's your life."

And that was the end of that conversation.

Later, with the help of my mom, I arranged for Daniel to meet my parents at a restaurant because it was neutral territory. He and my dad ended up talking for hours about business. My dad had started to invest in some real estate, so he had a lot of questions for Daniel. That was what broke the ice. Now my dad will call Daniel for legal advice and brags to all his friends that his son-in-law is a successful businessman and owns hotels.

By this time, I had also met Daniel's parents. They were very traditional Christian Koreans and had wanted Daniel to stay with his ex-wife for the sake of the kids and to keep their family unit together. Daniel was the youngest in his family but the first one to get divorced. Also, I think his parents really wanted him to remarry someone Korean because they don't speak much English. To this day, at all major family gatherings, Daniel's mom will look me in the eyes and speak Korean.

The first time it happened, about six months after we started dating, I said to Daniel, "Your mom knows I'm not Korean, right?"

"Yeah, of course she knows," he replied.

"Then why does she keep speaking to me in Korean?"

"You probably just look Korean to her, so she forgets that you're Chinese."

"That's lovely, but I can't understand a damn thing she's saying," I said. "I'm just sitting there smiling and nodding like an idiot."

"Just keep doing that, babe," he assured me. "It means she feels comfortable around you."

Maybe neither Daniel nor I are the people that our parents wanted their kids to end up with. Maybe we weren't that good together on paper, but we are good in real life.

AT THE END OF MY FIRST YEAR OF ANESTHESIA RESIDENCY, DANIEL flew out for the weekend to see me. One of our favorite getaways was Napa Valley, so he booked us a nice hotel room and made dinner reservations at the French Laundry. Being the maximizer that I am, I booked five wine tastings for us. (I was an amateur and now know that booking five tastings in one day is a wee bit aggressive.)

Our day started at 10 a.m. and ended around 6 p.m. Then we headed to dinner, where we had the tasting menu with wine pairings. I never thought I would say this, but at the end of the evening, I was all wined and dined out. I was still in the "it's blasphemy to spit" phase of my wine-tasting journey, and I drank just about every drop of wine that had been poured for me that day. It didn't seem like a lot at the time, but it quickly added up.

After we went back to our hotel room, Daniel started talking about how nice it was that we had a whole weekend together, just relaxing and enjoying each other's company and not having to work. Then, all of a sudden, he was down on one knee with a little velvet box in his hand with a sparkly diamond ring twinkling at me. Quite frankly, I thought that all the wine had gone to my head and I was hallucinating. I got lightheaded and felt like I was about to throw up.

I blubbered something incomprehensible but including the word *yes*, and he slipped the ring on my finger. I was officially engaged to the love of my life! I couldn't wait to tell my friends and especially my mom. *See, Mom, someone wants to marry me even though I don't cook.* (Daniel, by the way, does all the cooking at home.)

One of the things Daniel and I immediately agreed on was that we didn't want our wedding to be in Dallas. If it was in Dallas, our parents would invite all of their friends, and we wanted this moment to be just about us and *our* closest friends and family. At first we were thinking of getting married in Napa, but since I had relatives coming from China, we decided to get married in Hawaii, which was about halfway. It was the perfect place for a fresh start.

We got married the same year I finished my residency. After the wedding, I went to the Social Security office to change my name.

The agent was in disbelief. "You mean to tell me that your name is Tiffany Sun. And now you're changing it to Tiffany Moon?"

"Yes, sir," I replied.

"Well, then, it must have been written in the stars!"

We had a good laugh about it. I don't believe in predestination, especially when it comes to love. Sun and Moon are fairly common Chinese and Korean last names, and of course they don't have related meanings in those languages. But in some way, I can't help but think our future was preordained and that in fact, it was written in the stars for us.

Back in Dallas, I was enjoying my new life as a faculty member. I didn't even interview for any other jobs—this was the job of my dreams, practicing anesthesia while teaching residents and medical students and performing clinical research. It was also nice to receive my first attending paycheck and start paying down some of my student loans. My parents had always told me that my first paycheck belonged to them, but I wanted to exceed their expectations, so I bought my mom a brand-new Porsche Cayenne. I invited her over to my home to surprise her with it, big red bow on the hood and all.

In addition to work, I was enjoying my newlywed life. Having been apart for most of our relationship, Daniel and I appreciated finally being in the same city and sleeping in the same bed. One night we were watching a documentary on Netflix called *Jiro Dreams of Sushi*. It's about an eighty-year-old sushi chef in Tokyo who loves what he does so much that even at night, he dreams about making sushi. I was inspired by Jiro's dedication to his craft—buying only the most premium rice from a specific supplier in Japan, massaging an octopus for hours to make it tender, and teaching his two sons to carry on his legacy. I wanted to feel that same passion for my career.

"Wouldn't it be amazing if we could go to Japan and eat his sushi?" I said to Daniel.

"Yes, that would be amazing," he responded. "But if you really want to go, we should probably make plans sooner than later, because isn't he already eighty years old?"

"You have a point there. But when are we going to go? You know I'm not allowed to take vacation during the first six months of my job."

"Don't you have a three-day weekend coming up?"

So just like that, we made plans to go eat at Jiro's and explore Tokyo for a few days—two, to be exact, since the flight itself took a day.

I called in a favor from a Japanese friend I'd met at UCSF, and luckily, he was able to call and get us reservations.

Jiro's restaurant was tiny—a ten-seat restaurant under a subway station in the middle of Tokyo. The whole meal took about thirty minutes from start to finish (or did it just seem fast to me because I was having so much fun?). But it was the best damn sushi I've ever had in my life. You know how drug addicts will sometimes describe their first time getting high and say that every time after that, they're chasing the same feeling? Well, that was how I felt when I ate Jiro's sushi. I've been chasing that sushi high to this day.

Everything was so fresh. The shrimp was literally plucked live out of a bowl and deshelled in front of me. I felt bad for the shrimp, but that was the sweetest and most tender shrimp I've ever had in my life. Everything was prepared deliberately and with such care. You had to pick the sushi up with your hand and eat it without wasabi or soy sauce, just as it was prepared by Jiro. And you had to eat it as soon as it arrived. The only problem was that Daniel, who likes to take his time with his food, ate so slowly that Jiro scolded him for letting the sushi sit too long.

Five years earlier, Daniel and I had gone on our first date for sushi at Nobu. And now we were married, sitting at a restaurant in Tokyo, eating sushi made by one of the best sushi chefs in the world. All this would never have happened if I hadn't opened my heart to someone who, on paper, was not a good fit for me.

In many things, especially when it comes to love, it can be a good idea to put aside what you think *should* happen and open yourself up to what *could* happen. My parents had the preconceived notion that someone who was a different ethnicity, older, divorced, and with kids was not a good match for me. Honestly, these things were not what I would have chosen for myself either. If I had been on Match.com and one of the choices had been "previously married," I wouldn't have checked that box, and I would have missed out on the opportunity to be with a wonderful man. That aspect of Daniel's life did complicate our relationship, but it also showed me that we could work through challenges together. In a way, that brought us even closer together.

If I had stuck to my checklist of what I wanted in a potential mate, I might be married to (or divorced from) a Chinese doctor around my age who had never been married before. Sure, he might be able to speak to my parents in their native language, but could he really speak to my heart? I've learned since then that when it comes to relationships, you can't use a checklist to guide you—not in the beginning when you're getting to know someone or later when you're deciding whether you want to be together long term or start a family. What's good on paper may not be good for *you*. What's really good for you is taking the time to find out what you really want in a partner, especially if you intend it to be for life.

JOY PRESCRIPTION

Be Open to Love in Unexpected Places

- *Make connections in real life.* With today's dating apps, you can choose personality traits like items off a menu. But there is something to be said for making a meaningful connection with someone and getting to know them in person. Look up from your phone in the elevator or the next time you're at the grocery store and smile at that cute stranger looking at you.
- *Follow your own instincts.* At some point, you may be unsure of yourself and look to family or friends for advice. Ask yourself, are they being supportive, or are their own biases getting in the way? If it's the latter, think about whether you should listen to them or rely on your own instincts. No one knows you better than you.
- *Grow together.* Many times relationships don't work out because people grow apart. You don't need to have all the same interests as the other person, but you need to be able to grow together and support each other. This usually happens when you share the same fundamental values and want the same things out of life.

PART II

CHAPTER 5

UNCHARTED TERRITORY

Thirty-six weeks pregnant with twins

W HEN ASKED WHAT SHE WANTS TO BE WHEN SHE GROWS UP, no little girl ever answers, "A stepmom." A mom, a teacher, an astronaut, president of the United States... but never a stepmom. There's no national holiday called Stepmother's Day when stepmoms are treated to brunch, flowers, and cards.

Until I married Daniel and became a stepmom to his twins, Nathan and Nicole, my knowledge of stepmoms was based on exactly two things: the story of Cinderella and the tear-jerker movie

Stepmom starring Julia Roberts and Susan Sarandon. Since I was not interested in being the evil stepmother and my husband's ex-wife was not dying of cancer, these didn't provide me with many guidelines on how I should act.

After Daniel and I got married, I did what I always do when faced with an issue I don't know much about—I went out and bought a couple of books about how to become a stepmother with humor and grace. From these books, online reading, and my own experiences, I learned to act more like an aunt than a mom; to apply the phrase "Happy Wife, Happy Life" to the ex-wife as well; and, most of all, to not take things personally (this is much easier said than done).

From the beginning, I suspected that one of the most difficult aspects of our relationship would be the fact that Daniel had been previously married and that he and his ex-wife coparented their kids, who were four years old when Daniel and I met. It would have been much easier if he had been a widower as in *Stepmom*. Then I would have revered his ex-wife, put her on a pedestal, and honored her at every family gathering. We'd have kept a picture of her on the mantelpiece and placed flowers on her grave while I looked off into the distance with tears in my eyes. Just like Julia Roberts.

However, Daniel's ex-wife was very much alive, and I was constantly reminded of her presence. Before Daniel and I got married, I would see his twins about once every three months when I came back to Dallas from San Francisco. After I moved back to Dallas and we got married, I saw the kids every other week. When they were over, I tried my best to plan family activities, like going to the movies, arcade, bowling alley, and minigolf course. I remembered their favorite dishes at restaurants and what extracurriculars and hobbies they were interested in. I played with them, helped with homework, read to them, and generally tried to be another supportive adult in their life (without taking the place of their mom). Some days were great, and I felt warm and fuzzy inside when I thought about our little family. Other days I was reminded that I was an outsider, and I worried that I might never fit in.

Once, when I was making them ham-and-cheese sandwiches, Nathan blurted out, "That's not the way my mom does it."

"Oh, how does she do it?" I asked.

"She cuts it into rectangles, not triangles," he said between mouthfuls of the offending sandwich. "And she toasts the bread first."

My first instinct was to blurt out, "Well I'm not trying to be like your mom," but instead I forced a smile onto my face and said, "Okay, I'll try to remember that for next time."

It was frustrating because I was trying my best, but I just knew that every mistake I made was being reported back to their mom and used as ammunition against me: "You mean she didn't even toast the bread before she made your sandwich? She just made it on cold bread?" And then the three of them would laugh.

I tried to be understanding and see things from her point of view. *Her husband wants a divorce. He moves out and starts a new life. She has to coordinate their kids' drop-off and pickup schedule and extracurricular activities with him. She gets her kids on Thanksgiving or Christmas, but not both. Then one day her ex-husband tells her that he's seeing someone and it's becoming serious . . . but who is this new person?*

I could imagine where Daniel's ex was coming from and felt bad for her, but I hadn't caused their divorce, and I was just trying to be another loving adult figure in the kids' lives. Quite frankly, if she had asked me to submit a driving-record check, background check, and credit report, I would gladly have done it to give her peace of mind. Yes, I know those things don't equate to being a good parent, but I was responsible and caring and wanted the best for the kids. I wanted her to know that I wasn't trying to take her place or diminish her role as their mother. I wanted to be an ally, but it's hard to do that when the other person wants you to be an enemy.

Once, about a year after we got married, Daniel and I took Nathan and Nicole on vacation to Florida. Daniel chartered a boat for us to go snorkeling and fishing. The day we went, the weather was so windy that our faces started to turn green as the boat rocked back and forth in the water. Daniel tried to make it fun and exciting, like a scene from a Disney movie, but the kids and I were not having it—we just wanted to get back on dry land. At one point, Nicole grabbed my hand and wouldn't let go.

When we got off the boat, she dropped my hand and turned to me, her eyes dark with worry. "Please don't tell my mom that we held hands," she said. "She'll get mad at me."

First of all, she didn't need to worry that I would say anything to her mom because the two of us never talked privately. My second reaction was sadness that Nicole was only nine years old but already caught between following her mother's instructions and becoming closer to her stepmom. I was disheartened that she thought if she let me just a little bit into her heart, her mother would consider it a betrayal. Before that, whenever the children were being difficult, I just figured they were "being kids" or didn't like me. However, I began to wonder if, consciously or subconsciously, they were receiving signals that being nice to me or liking me was an affront to their mother.

In our newlywed days, Daniel and I had some issues to work out, just like any other couple. We had spent the vast majority of our relationship living thousands of miles apart, so there were some adjustments once we moved in together. However, rather than arguments about money, housework, or any number of things that people typically fight about, our arguments were mostly over his kids. Not because of *them* personally but because of how he parented them.

Generally I tried not to interfere with his parenting, but there were some instances when I just felt the need to speak up. For example, the kids were in the habit of eating snacks and watching TV in bed before going to sleep. On more than one occasion, I found them asleep with the TV still on and half-eaten cookies in their hands, melted chocolate chips staining the sheets. Being a doctor, I found a few scientific articles supporting my claim that it's best for children not to have a TV in their bedroom, or at least to limit its use before bedtime.

I took the articles to Daniel and said, "I don't think we should allow the kids to watch TV right before bed. Research shows that the blue light from the TV can disrupt their circadian rhythm, and I think they would go to sleep sooner if the TV wasn't on."

Before I could even get to the ant problem I'd discovered in their bedroom because of the late-night snacking, Daniel said, "This is what they do at their mom's house. They have a snack and watch TV until they fall asleep."

"Last time I checked, this isn't their mom's house," I pointed out. "This is our house. Our house, which now has an ant problem. Different houses have different rules, so maybe we should be more clear about our expectations here."

"There's a lot that's different for them now. I'd like to keep some things the same," Daniel replied. That hadn't occurred to me, and I felt bad that I hadn't really looked at it that way before. In the grand scheme of things, none of these little issues actually mattered, and I reminded myself that I needed to focus on providing the kids with comfort and consistency in the midst of all these changes.

Another time we went to the fair, and the kids wanted to get ice cream. Each of them chose three flavors. About halfway into each scoop, Nicole stated, "I'm done," and tossed her half-eaten ice cream into a trash can.

"Why did you order three scoops if you weren't going to eat them?" I asked, genuinely curious.

"I just wanted to try more flavors. I wasn't planning on finishing it," she replied nonchalantly.

I was flabbergasted. "Well, if you're not that hungry, maybe it's best to just choose one or two flavors and finish the whole thing and save the other flavor to try next time," I said to her.

I was trying to be matter-of-fact and not condescending, but when I looked at Daniel, he stared at me as if I'd grown a third eyeball on my forehead. "Relax, it's just ice cream," he said curtly.

Having grown up in a world of scarcity, I found the idea of throwing ice cream away unimaginable. In the rare event that I was given a treat as a child, you better bet I finished every last bite of it. I wasn't upset with the kids per se; I was upset at Daniel. I was worried that the message he was sending them was that if you have the means, it's okay to be wasteful.

There was so much more I wanted to say, but I bit my tongue. I knew a lot of what I felt came from the way *I* had been brought up, and I was projecting my own childhood issues onto them. The kids were already having to deal with so much confusion and upheaval in their lives. Their dad had chosen me, but *they* hadn't. I wanted to be conscious of and empathetic about that.

And of course our arguments weren't *actually* about the blue light from the TV, crumbs in the bed, and wasted ice cream. It was about me feeling like an outsider in my own home and feeling like I had no jurisdiction. I understood that Daniel and his kids had little habits and traditions that the three of them had developed over the years together. I could also see things from Daniel's perspective— the immense guilt he must feel about spending only part of the time with his kids. As much as he wanted to, he could never be with them 100 percent of the time. More than once, I overheard the kids asking why they couldn't see him every day, and I saw how sad they were when it was time to go back to their mom's house. That must have really torn him up, but I didn't ask him about it because I didn't want to highlight a problem that didn't have a solution. I wanted to give him the space to preserve his relationship with them, to maintain their closeness, and to minimize the disruption to their lives.

In the beginning, I was frustrated because this was not a situation that I had encountered (or even imagined) before. Previously I'd had three main ways of dealing with a problem: asking my friends for advice, researching the solution in books, or ignoring it altogether. The advice that my friends could offer was limited since none of them had ex-wives to deal with or were stepmoms. I couldn't exactly ignore the problem, and despite my best efforts, there was no book called *How to Marry a Divorced Man, Coparent His Kids, and Deal with His Difficult Ex-Wife.* Usually I could research my way out of a problem, but it wasn't going to be so easy this time.

In an interesting twist of fate, a few years later, Daniel's ex-wife married Daniel's brother's wife's brother (I guess she really wanted to stay in the family). She then became a stepmom herself, with her husband's ex-wife to deal with. I don't know if this made her any more sympathetic to my struggles—we still do not talk privately—but at least I know she has a glimpse of what it's like on the other side.

Today Nathan and Nicole are well-adjusted adults with their own lives. When they come home during breaks from college, we catch up on things like dating, school, and future career plans. My girls are ecstatic to see their big brother and sister, and each year we all try to take a family vacation together. It's not what I would have imagined my family would look like when I was twenty, but it is my family, and I love the way it all turned out. Through this experience, I learned a lot about being a parent, picking your battles, and having patience. I also learned that, try as I might, there are some things in life that are outside my control, and I need to be able to let these things go in order to move forward.

These new skills would come in handy much sooner than I realized.

⌒

WHEN YOU ARE A BOX CHECKER, WHAT COMES AFTER MARRIAGE? For me, as for many women, it was getting pregnant. Even though Daniel and I had been married for only six months, my Chinese aunties were already asking me, "Are you pregnant yet?" Every time she saw me, my mom dropped hints about a grandchild. "You know, I was twenty-five years old when you were born," she said. "How old are you now—twenty-nine?"

I retorted, "Well, you weren't a board-certified anesthesiologist, were you?" The truth was, Daniel and I were trying, and nothing was happening.

I had imagined that getting pregnant would be easy. I had worked around obstetricians for years, and my friends seemed to be conceiving with no trouble. I had gone to dozens of baby showers and oohed and aahed over every cute little outfit and miniature pair of booties. I thought I had built up good baby-making karma. I wasn't even thirty yet, nowhere near being called a "geriatric" mother (nothing is more ageist than the fertility industry). I expected it to be a sure thing, just another box to check off. Instead, I found out that it was a lot of work.

First off, there is nothing fun about having sex if you're doing it to get pregnant. I was so obsessed with getting pregnant that I peed on an ovulation strip each morning and stuck it into a little machine that showed one, two, or three bars. If it was a one-bar day, I had no interest. "Not today, honey, just one bar," I would tell Daniel. As soon as I got two bars, I'd be making dinner reservations at some romantic restaurant, knowing that three bars would happen soon. There was a science to getting pregnant, and science was my thing. But all that scientific knowledge wasn't helping me one bit here. You know women who seem to get pregnant if they sneeze? Well, that was not me.

Finally, after a year of trying, I got pregnant. I knew it because I took three separate pregnancy tests from three different brands—you know, just to be sure. One had a control line and a solid test line, one had a plus sign, and one actually spelled out the word *pregnant*. I was ecstatic—we'd finally done it. I called Daniel immediately, and he was overjoyed, excited to be a father again. We started brainstorming about what we would name the baby if it was a boy versus a girl and joked that our dogs would become *chan bap* (which literally translates to "cold rice" in Korean) once the baby came. I was pretty nauseated the first two months, so my OB prescribed Zofran, which worked like a charm. I continued my normal work schedule, which included one twenty-four-hour call per month.

While in surgery one day, still in my first trimester, I felt that something was off. After we had the patient safely extubated, I let my resident take him to the recovery room while I went to the restroom. I called my OB and told her I had some bleeding.

"Do you think it'll matter if I come now or after I finish this next case?"

"You need to come now" was her answer.

So I left one hospital and went to another, transitioning from being the doctor to being the patient. There my OB confirmed that I was miscarrying while I sobbed and called Daniel. Even though my OB assured me that the miscarriage was not my fault, I blamed myself. Had I been working too much? Should I have been drinking more water? Should I not have gone jogging the day before? *No*, my OB told me, *jogging was not the cause.*

Daniel and I gave ourselves some time to grieve and to let my body heal before trying again. I was sad but also scared and anxious. What if it happened again? Or what if something was wrong with me and I was never able to have children? Would Daniel leave me? I have a tendency to catastrophize, and my mind went crazy doing exactly that. After the miscarriage, my OB did some additional testing and diagnosed me with polycystic ovary syndrome (PCOS), a common hormonal issue that happens to women of childbearing age. I had learned about PCOS in medical school—it usually presented with signs such as excess body hair, obesity, or acne. I had none of those things, so my PCOS was deemed "atypical." Then I learned something even more disturbing—I had a cyst the size of a grapefruit on one of my ovaries. I weighed maybe one hundred pounds at the time, yet I had a growth the size of a large citrus fruit in my body, and *I had no clue.* So in a way, something useful came out of my miscarriage because otherwise I wouldn't have found out about the PCOS and ovarian cyst, which I had to have surgically removed.

Getting pregnant was not going to be the walk in the park that I had expected. For so long I'd assumed that I had complete control over my body—that because I could keep from getting pregnant when I didn't want to, I could get pregnant when I wanted to—but that was far from the truth. As a doctor, you think you know everything about your body and how it works. I can draw you a diagram of the menstrual cycle—the follicular versus the luteal phase and how the levels of each hormone should fluctuate. Yet I had no idea what was going on with my own body, and I had even less control over it. Although I knew so much about the human body, none of that knowledge was helping me get pregnant.

As a doctor, when I look at a patient's chart, I can tell certain things about them: their medical problems, medications, and past surgical history. Everything is clearly marked and delineated. Most of the time, looking at a patient's chart can give you a fairly decent idea of what's wrong with them and how they should be treated. But a chart doesn't tell you other important things, like what happened in someone's past and how they're feeling.

Previously my medical chart had been pristine, but now it was a mess. *Infertility...miscarriage...PCOS...ovarian cyst necessitating surgical removal...* the list went on. And then there were the things that couldn't be written down on a chart but were very much present. Like how guilty I felt about the miscarriage, how worried I was that I wouldn't be able to get pregnant again, and my sense of shame that this was something so simple, but I could not do it. I was literally in uncharted territory.

Usually I dealt with my anxiety by doubling down on work, but that couldn't be the solution this time. I was still convinced that working too hard and being stressed had contributed to my miscarriage, so I decided to cut back on my hours. Instead of taking my usual twenty-four-hour trauma call, I split it into two twelve-hour calls on different weekends. I was already thinking ahead to how much time I'd be able to take off for maternity leave. Of course I'd want to work until the last possible minute before giving birth to show my superiors that I took my job seriously and that I wasn't going to let something as silly as childbearing interfere with my career.

About six months after I had surgery to remove my ovarian cyst, I discovered that I was pregnant again. I didn't tell anyone because I was frightened that I would have another miscarriage. At my seven-week ultrasound, the sonographer hesitated as she looked at the screen. I knew something was not normal. *No, please, not bad news again*, I thought. I turned my head slowly so that I could see the screen, and I saw two black circles with a little flicker inside each. *I was pregnant with twins.*

I took a picture of the ultrasound on my phone and texted it to Daniel.

You're kidding me, he texted back.

When I called Lisa to tell her, she exclaimed, "Wow, Tiff, even your ovaries are overachievers!" *Wow, I guess they are*, I thought, proud of my ovaries and scared shitless at the same time.

At sixteen weeks, Daniel and I found out that we were having twin girls. We started discussing potential names. I knew that I wanted their middle names to be my maiden name, Sun.

"What if we call the girls Star and Sky?" I asked Daniel excitedly. "Aren't those such cute girl names? We could even spell them *Starr* and *Skye*."

"Ummm, those sound like stripper names," he objected.

"What's wrong with strippers? They're hardworking and providing a service for a fee."

So back to the drawing board we went for baby names. Joking aside, I knew all too well from my years working in the hospital what could go wrong with twins. They could be born too early, need to be in the NICU for weeks, and have lifelong complications as a result of their prematurity. In general, knowing more about a situation helped because I always found comfort in knowledge. But here, medically and anecdotally, I knew too much. I couldn't stop thinking about the worst that could happen.

Then something did happen. One morning, around thirty weeks, I had some spotting and called my OB. After I went to see her and she checked my cervix, she said, "I'm admitting you to the hospital. Your cervix is dilated."

But it's too early! I thought. *I've been following the rules. I cut back on work, and I even stopped jogging. This can't be happening.*

After a week on bed rest in the hospital and daily ultrasounds to check on the babies and my fluid levels, I was allowed to go home.

But I had to stay on bed rest for the next six weeks to try to keep my babies from being born too early. I had to call my boss to say that I was starting my maternity leave, effective immediately. I apologized profusely for this (as if I had any control) and said I would "make up for it" later when I came back to work (I don't even know what I meant by that).

I was on "modified bed rest," which meant that I could get up to use the restroom, eat, and shower, but that was it. Prescribing bed rest to someone as active as I am is absolute torture. While on bed rest, I had a lot of time to think. You may have heard about postpartum depression, but I think I had *pre*partum depression. I tried to watch TV and read, but all I could think about were my girls and how if I couldn't keep them in long enough, I would be failing them. My anxiety was crippling. My bad habit of catastrophizing was in full swing, and I kept picturing very dark scenarios. Every morning I woke up grateful to still be pregnant. Each week Daniel drove me to my maternal fetal medicine specialist, where he would go inside the hospital and call for a wheelchair so I could minimize the number of steps I took. In eight months, I had ballooned from 105 to 165 pounds—my body ached, the only shoes I could wear were flip-flops, and I was short of breath anytime I walked more than ten steps.

At night I couldn't sleep—it was July in Texas, with daily highs in the 100s. I was perpetually hot, and no position was comfortable. I tossed and turned all night while Daniel snored softly beside me. "Do you need to make it so cold in here?" he said one evening. I gave him a death stare that only pregnant women are capable of, and Daniel slunk out of the room and came back wearing his flannel PJs.

My OB told me, "The best thing you can do for your girls is to relax. They can sense your stress, worry, and anxiety. Increasing your cortisol levels is only going to exacerbate the problem. Why don't you try to watch a funny movie or read a book?"

"I've already rewatched the entire *Sex and the City* series and read all the books about what to expect when you're expecting. Is there anything else I can do?" I asked frantically.

Previously my escape mechanism had been to work, but now I didn't have that. The intrusive thoughts started to come fast and thick.

> *What if my girls were born too early?*
> *What if they had breathing problems their entire lives because*
> *their lungs didn't have time to develop?*
> *Would I be a good mother?*

I tried my best to distract myself from these worries. Daniel was busy with work, so I'd ask my friends to drop by with bubble tea, fried chicken, or whatever my pregnancy craving of the day was. I called some old friends to catch up over the phone (even though I generally don't enjoy talking on the phone).

Another of my OB's suggestions was to pick up a hobby. I had always wanted to learn photography, so Daniel got me a brand-new digital camera. I figured that if I learned to be a decent photographer, when the girls were born, I could take all their photos instead of hiring someone. I hadn't considered how difficult and mundane it would be to learn photography while confined to bed. After countless pictures of my feet, my dogs, and the vase of flowers on the dresser, I decided now wasn't the time to learn.

When my thirtieth birthday rolled around, Daniel said he wanted to do something special for me, but it was difficult to plan much with me being on bed rest and all. By then I was close to thirty-five weeks, which my doctor said was generally "out of the woods" in terms of the babies needing to go to the NICU. Daniel surprised me with a trip to my favorite store, Hermès. He had arranged for an appointment with my favorite sales associate, who booked a private room that he filled with things he thought I might like. I got to sit down (still abiding by my modified-bed-rest orders) while I looked at all the beautiful jewelry and bags they'd selected for me.

Two weeks later, I gave birth to beautiful twin girls who weighed almost six pounds each. Less than twenty-four hours after delivery, I was home with my babies. I felt like my worrying had paid off, but that only freed me up to worry about new things. Would I make enough milk to feed two mouths? Could I remember how to properly swaddle a baby? I had read so many books, but all that knowledge seemed to have mysteriously vanished from my brain. How was I going to take care of these little human beings? What I didn't realize was that my fears weren't just about what would happen to my babies—my fears were about the loss of control. And this fear was deeply rooted in the way I had grown up.

Growing up, I had no control over anything in my life—my parents leaving me behind in China when I was just three years old, being taken away from my grandparents to move to America, moving every few years in the middle of a school year, wishing for a sibling for so long and then getting one four years before I moved out of the house. In school, I was always the planner for group projects. When I became an adult, I planned every step of my life. And my career? Well, what gives you more control than being an anesthesiologist? I always have a plan A, B, and C for everything. While this takes up a lot of mental bandwidth, it also brings me comfort and soothes my anxiety. I call it the vicious circle of anxiety:

- Worry about everything and make multiple contingency plans for if anything goes awry.

- Usually something goes awry.
- This reinforces the practice of worrying and needing to be prepared.

Is it exhausting? *Yes.* Do I know any other way to be? *No.*

But when it came time for me to have kids, nothing went the way I had planned. I had trouble getting pregnant, experienced a miscarriage, and had to go on bed rest for six weeks. Even though I was a doctor—and in my work I controlled when people went to sleep and when they woke up, what their blood pressure and heart rate were, and how many breaths per minute they took—I couldn't control what was going on with my own body.

Why was it such a struggle for me to give up control? I always wanted to *make* things happen instead of *allowing* them to happen. I once read that the root of control is fear. That made complete sense to me. It was as if I worked so hard to control things because I was afraid that if I didn't, something bad would happen. But here I was, working furiously to try to control everything, and the universe kept throwing me curveballs. The thing about trying to be in control all the time is that it is utterly exhausting. Not only are you constantly anxious, but planning for every single thing that could possibly go wrong and how you would handle it leaves very little room to be present, enjoy the moment, and relax. The more I tried to be *in control*, the more things spiraled *out of control* until I realized that if I didn't learn how to surrender, I would be on a path of self-destruction. I realized that in trying to control my life, my steadfast grip on it was squeezing out all the spontaneity and creativity. The very thing I wanted so badly—joy—was being suffocated by my own doing.

It's not like one day I just decided it would be better for my stress levels if I just relinquished control, and my brain agreed to just chill out. Since I had been a lifelong control freak, it took some major work to teach myself the art of surrender—but if I can do it, you can too. The thing that helped me most was knowing that whatever happened in the future, I had the aptitude and attitude to deal with it. I didn't just completely surrender and say, "Okay, I guess whatever happens happens." Instead, I told myself, "Sometimes life takes twists and turns, but I trust myself to have the insight and judgment to deal with whatever may arise."

Letting go of control also helped me to be more satisfied with life. My therapist once told me that happiness = reality − expectations. With my need to be in control, I had high expectations for things. (How could I not after all the worrying I'd put into it, even if all that work was in my head?) When reality didn't measure up, I was often disappointed, sad, or confused. Letting go of control allowed me to lower my expectations and shift my equation toward more happiness.

Sometimes, in order to handle the curveballs that life throws, you need to take a step back, look at the way you've dealt with things in the past, and make a new plan for the future that involves letting go of what you can't control. When you do that, you just might be amazed at what you're capable of.

JOY PRESCRIPTION

Accept What You Can't Control and Focus on What You Can

- *Instead of fighting to control every aspect of your life, try to relax and let some of those things go.* Is stressing about the problem doing any good? Probably not. Try to find a healthy outlet for your stress—talk to a friend or a therapist, exercise, meditate. At the same time, recognize that there are some things you *do* have a say over. Lean in to these things to help you create a sense of stability as you navigate this new terrain.

- *Remind yourself of what you've overcome.* Draw from your own experiences and how you've successfully navigated difficult situations in the past. Be confident that you have the insight, judgment, and wisdom to overcome the adversities that arise.

- *Reach out to other people for advice.* Recognize that you don't have to go it alone. There may be others in your life—friends, relatives, coworkers—who have gone through similar challenges. Sometimes listening to other people talk about their challenges and how they overcame them can help you deal with what you're going through. It can give you perspective and confidence that you can get through this too.

CHAPTER 6

YES-WOMAN

Me with my twin girls

THE ALARM RANG. BLEARY-EYED, I GOT UP TO BREASTFEED THE twins. After feeding one, I put her back into the crib and went to use the bathroom. When I returned, I could not for the life of me remember which of them I'd just fed. Was it Chloe or Maddie? They both slept quietly as I stood there, paralyzed with confusion and exhaustion. Figuring I had a fifty-fifty chance of getting it right, I picked up Maddie and tried to feed her, but she wouldn't latch and started crying. So I put her down and tried Chloe, but she started crying too. It was 3 a.m., and I had two crying babies, one who was fed and one who was not, but I didn't know which was which. I sat down in the recliner and started crying too.

You might already know that the United States is the only developed nation that doesn't have mandatory paid maternity leave. This means new moms have to choose between their jobs and, essentially, recovering from childbirth and taking care of their children. Yeah, that's bullshit. Women are expected to raise children as if they don't work, and they're expected to work as if they don't have children. We exalt mothers, put them on a pedestal—we're told that being a mother is the most important "job" we could ever have—yet there's no sick leave, no overtime, and no pay. If this were an actual job description, who would apply?

While I don't have many regrets in life, if I could do it over, I would do that first year of motherhood differently. Six weeks before giving birth, I was on bed rest, and six weeks after giving birth, I was back at work—full-time plus taking overnight trauma call and liver transplant call and acting as principal investigator for multiple clinical trials. I was working sixty hours a week in the hospital and frequently worked at home as well. I distinctly remember breastfeeding with one arm and editing a manuscript with the other. On one occasion, I worked all day, went home for a few hours, and then got called back in to do a liver transplant, which lasted from 8 p.m. to 6 a.m. Then at 6 a.m., I took a shower, changed scrubs, and went from one hospital to another, where I worked another full day until 5 p.m. I was delirious, but I wanted to prove that being a good doctor and a good mom were not mutually exclusive. I had seen coworkers take personal leave or go part-time, and when they came back (if they ever came back), they were on a different career trajectory. *That wasn't going to happen to me*, I thought. I hadn't worked my ass off in medical school and residency just to give it all up once I became a mom. So I went back to work, full steam ahead, never mind that I had pushed two humans out of my body just six weeks earlier.

In order to keep my milk supply up (I had two mouths to feed, after all), I had an app with an alarm that went off every three hours, reminding me to pump. At work, the only private place was the women's locker room, so I'd sit on the floor of the shower stall to pump while eating lactation cookies, guzzling water, and answering emails. When the girls were three months old, I traveled to Chicago for a conference, where I went to my room every three hours to pump. At the airport, when I opened my carry-on to show the TSA agent the dozens of plastic bags filled with breast milk, she said, "Damn, honey, that's a lot of milk!" I told her, "Yeah, I'm basically a milk machine."

Pumping was my way of showing my dedication to motherhood. I was obsessed with my daily output, logging how much milk I made in the app on my phone. If I didn't get at least forty ounces a day, I berated myself for not drinking enough water or for forgetting my fenugreek supplement (which makes your burps smell absolutely horrible). I ran that nursery the only way I knew how—like an operating room. I had a chart with strict ins and outs, hourly notes on each twin, and sleep and wake times. I'm not kidding—I made a spreadsheet template, printed out multiple copies, hole-punched them, and put them into a binder, one sheet for each day. I even logged everything in military time like we do at the hospital, except one night I was so tired I wrote, *25:30 Breastfed 20 min each, burped, changed diaper.* Later, my nanny asked, "What time is 25:30?" to which I replied, "It's 1:30 a.m. when I've been up since the previous day and haven't slept."

I don't think I slept for longer than three hours at a time the first six months after giving birth. Not long ago someone's phone alarm went off with the exact sound I used for breastfeeding alarms, and

I swear my nipples tingled a bit—it was like a Pavlovian response. A dog hears a bell and salivates because food is coming. I hear an iPhone alarm, and my mind flashes back to the sucking sound of the breast pump and chapped nipples.

In retrospect, I'm pretty sure I had postpartum depression. But at the time, I refused to acknowledge it, let alone seek treatment. Instead, I leaned in to work. Overachievement had always been my coping mechanism, and it was coming out in full force here, no matter the cost to my physical and mental health. As my daughters grew, the dual expectations from my job and motherhood made work-life balance pretty much impossible. When one-half of the equation was doing well, it generally meant the other half wasn't. I started asking myself whether it was really possible to "have it all."

⌒

ONE OF THE TIMES I REMEMBER FEELING MOST CONFLICTED between my work life and personal life was when I missed Chloe's first steps.

The twins were a little over a year old by this point, and we had a full-time nanny. I usually left for work at 6:15, so I didn't see the girls most mornings. One day while working, I got a text from the nanny. I thought something was wrong since she didn't normally text me at work, but it was a video with the message "Look at this!" *It was Chloe taking her first steps.* But what should have been a moment of joy was a moment of sadness for me.

I had missed it.

I should have been there.

What other milestones would I miss?

Was I a bad mom?

But I couldn't dwell on it for long because I had ten minutes before I had to get my next patient into the operating room lest I get dinged for having a long turnover time (ORs don't make money when they're empty). I had to pull up my big-girl panties, wipe my eyes, and put a smile on my face to go greet my next patient.

Even when I was with the girls, I was reminded of all the time I spent away from them. I'll never forget the day two-year-old Maddie scraped her knee at the playground and started to cry. I ran to her and started to comfort her, but she pushed me away while screaming for the nanny. It was a dagger to my heart. But how was I going to spend more time with them when their waking hours were 7 a.m. to 7 p.m. and I was generally gone from 6:30 a.m. to 5 p.m. at least five days a week?

Soon I devised a way to spend more time with my kids *and* keep up my productivity at work. Every night there was an on-call anesthesiologist who did the emergency cases. It was a 3 p.m. to 7 a.m. shift, and you had the whole next day "off." I signed up for as many of these overnight calls as possible. If I heard my colleagues complaining about having to take overnight call, I would volunteer to take theirs too. If I planned it right, I could get one to two overnight call shifts per week. The day before going to work was the best because I would spend the entire day with my girls, going to the park, zoo, or a mommy-and-me music or art class. I'd put them down for a nap around 1 p.m. and start getting ready for work. At the hospital, sometimes I got a few hours of sleep, but sometimes I didn't even see the inside of my call room. I'd get off at 7 a.m. and return home to wake up the girls and have breakfast with them. Then I would take a short nap and spend the rest of the afternoon and evening with my family. In this way, I was fulfilling all my obligations at work *and* at home (or so I thought).

The only problem was that I was a zombie. Working days and nights in the same week really messes with your circadian rhythm. I frequently didn't know what day it was. *Wait, it's Thursday already?*

I thought today was Wednesday. One day the girls had an end-of-year ballet recital on a Friday afternoon. To ensure that I could go, I signed up to take the overnight call on Thursday and was up all night doing emergency cases. Friday afternoon, I sat down in the auditorium and waited eagerly for their group. Well, I never saw them come onstage because I fell asleep. The next thing I knew, the lights had come on and the other parents were shuffling out of their seats to go greet their dancers. I found the girls and gave them the mini–flower bouquets I had made and said, "Oh my gosh, girls, you did such an amazing job. Mommy is so proud of you!" But the truth was, I hadn't seen a damn thing.

Later, Daniel asked me, "Did you take any video?"

I lied, "Oh, my phone was dying and the lighting was so bad—I didn't get any good clips."

I felt like the biggest mom failure.

I had plenty of other videos and pictures of the girls on my phone—whenever we were out, I was sure to record these moments—but when I went back and looked at some of them, I would think, *I know I took this picture, but I cannot for the life of me remember that day.* Everything was a blur. I wasn't truly present at work or at home, but I didn't know what to do.

I reached out to my med school friends Lisa and Michelle, who both had kids by this time, to see how they handled this issue. They were also juggling work and motherhood, and they were supportive, but they didn't understand why I felt like I still needed to prove myself.

"Why don't you just cut back at work?" Michelle asked.

"Don't be so hard on yourself," Lisa said after I told her the story about missing Chloe's first steps. "It's not like your kids are going to remember you not being there. They're not going to end up in therapy just because their mom missed their first steps."

"They might!" I exclaimed.

Thinking back, though, I didn't remember anything about life in China with my mom before the age of three, which was when she and my dad left for America without me. However, I do recall when I was older wishing that my mom could stay home from work to be with me, especially around holidays and during the summer. I wasn't sure whether my mom had felt the same sense of inner conflict that I was feeling. When I told her that I was thinking of staying home with the girls, her response was "Don't quit. One day your kids will be older and leave the house, but you won't have a job, and you won't be able to get one because you haven't been working. If you quit, you'll throw away all your education and training." It was a catch-22.

Of course my mom hadn't had the luxury of opting to be a stay-at-home mom. She couldn't have made that choice if she wanted to put food on the table or keep a roof over our heads. I had that choice, but I *wanted* to go back to work after the girls were born—I liked taking care of patients, teaching residents and medical students, and running clinical trials. I thought that if I found someone who could take good care of my kids, I could continue to work, spend time with them whenever I wasn't working, and have the best of both worlds.

The truth was, *I loved my job.* If I hadn't, I would have quit with no qualms. And if I had quit, no one would have questioned me. When I was pregnant, people would say to me, "You're not going to go back to work, *are you?* With *twins?*" And I would reply, "Well, I was planning to." In my brain, it was all or nothing. There was no such thing as going part-time. Part-time to me was half-assed, and I didn't do anything half-assed. Plus, back when my girls were babies, part-time anesthesiology positions didn't really exist. Today things are different and there are more flexible, part-time positions available for anesthesiologists. At the time, less than 5 percent of the faculty anesthesiologists at my hospital were part-time. Almost all of them were women with families, and after they went part-time, I didn't see any of them advance to leadership positions and I'd hear colleagues refer to them as being on the "mommy track." My belief was that in the trajectory of your career, you were either rising or falling. The way it was in academic medicine, the first five years of your career were the most important because these years were your opportunity to demonstrate your potential and secure your position on the "rising star" trajectory rather than the "worker bee" trajectory. (My friends in law and investment banking tell me that there is a very similar belief in their fields.)

Back then I wasn't thinking about what happened once you reached the peak of that trajectory or if I even truly wanted that for myself. I couldn't see that far ahead yet. I hadn't stopped to consider that many people in leadership positions at my hospital seemed miserable. If I had considered this, I might have recognized that there are very few women in these top leadership positions in medicine because of reasons that range from work hours that are incompatible with raising a family to being overlooked for promotions that favor their male colleagues. According to the American Medical Women's Association, around 30 percent of women physicians leave full-time medicine within six years after finishing residency. With statistics like that, you have to wonder what kind of pressures women are under for them to give up or cut back on careers that they have worked so hard for.

I asked for career advice from a mentor who'd been in my department for almost twenty years. She had known me for a decade, since I was a medical student, and I trusted her.

"I'm really torn," I confided. "I want to be home with my kids, but not every day, all day. I love my career and want to practice, teach, and do research. But I also want to be there for my kids when they need me. Right now I feel like I'm running myself ragged trying to do everything, and I don't know how much longer I can last. Should I ask to go part-time?"

She gave me a look. "Do you want my honest answer, Tiffany?"
I nodded.

"With the path you're on and where I see you ending up, going part-time would be career suicide."

So I put that idea aside and soldiered on. I worked harder, took more call shifts, published more papers, and kept teaching and mentoring my medical students and residents. The problem was that there was simply not enough time in the day to be everything and do everything. Each day it felt like I was racing against the clock to do all the things I needed to get done. Also, the more time and effort I put in at work, the guiltier I felt about not spending more time at home. I didn't *have* to work (like my mom had when I was growing up); I was *choosing* to work. That just made me feel more guilty because it seemed like I was choosing my career over my family, though I wanted both. I was being pushed and pulled in all different directions, and I was exhausted.

Where was I in all this? Funny you should ask. My list of priorities in life went in this order:

- Be a good mom
- Be a good doctor
- Be a good wife
- Be a good daughter
- Be a good friend
- Be good to myself

Even if I got around to the last bullet, that goal was focused mostly on external improvements, such as exercising—not to improve my cardiovascular health but so I could lose the weight I'd gained during my pregnancy. A year after the twins were born, the only clothes I could fit into were my scrubs and yoga pants. Other women seemed to be popping out babies and then walking down the Victoria's Secret runway five weeks later. Certainly I should be able to fit back into my prebaby jeans by now, right?

When I was able to spare some time for myself, it was only for things that I felt would be productive. I reorganized the pantry so that things could be found more easily. I read parenting books and signed myself and the girls up for toddler gym and swimming classes. (I'd always regretted not knowing how to swim, so I was going to make darn sure my girls learned.) It did not even cross my mind to make time to care for myself or to address what was going on inside my head. In fact, it seemed almost selfish to focus on myself when all these other people needed me.

Has anyone ever told you, when you were going through a hard time, that you just needed to relax and practice better self-care? Buy a new face cream, meditate, or take a vacation? This sort of advice is well intentioned, and self-care practices like these are helpful— don't get me wrong—but they don't necessarily get to the root of our problems. And no wonder. You can't put a Band-Aid on a gaping wound and expect it to heal.

One day, after I received the Faculty of the Year teaching award, I was talking to a coworker, and she said, "Tiffany, you're totally killing it."

I smiled and nodded and said, "Gee, thanks," but what I really wanted to say was *And it's killing me.*

I was dying a slow death by my own sword, and I had no idea how to stop the bleeding. It felt like I was on a treadmill and someone was increasing the speed, but *I could not get off.* To stop, I was going to have to break my foot, or someone was going to have to push me off.

Warren Buffett is quoted as saying that the difference between successful people and really successful people is that really successful people say no to almost everything. That was the complete opposite of my life philosophy at the time. I was a yes-woman. After all, saying yes had gotten me to where I was in life. I'd said yes to my early college program, yes to medical school, yes to a competitive and challenging residency program, and yes to taking on extra assignments at work. I said yes to everything.

Tiffany, can you be in charge of the thoracic anesthesia service?

Yes.

Tiffany, can you plan Emily's baby shower?

Yes.

Mommy, can you sleep on the floor in our room so the monsters don't come?

Yes.

Babe, can you call the plumber to fix the toilet in the guest room?

Yes.

I knew I had a choice. I could say no to any and all these things, but I was afraid that if I did, I would disappoint someone. My boss might think that I wasn't dedicated to my job. Someone might think I wasn't a good friend. My kids would think I didn't care enough about them. My next overnight guest wouldn't be able to use the toilet—and all of it would be my fault.

I felt that if I didn't say yes, especially when it came to my career, not only would I disappoint people, but I would lose an opportunity to demonstrate my worthiness. I have since come to recognize that people who can say no comfortably are able to do so because they don't base their self-worth on how useful they are to others. Instead, they simply believe in their worthiness, knowing that they're a good friend without having to demonstrate it all the time or that they're good at their job without volunteering for every extra assignment.

I struggled with self-worth, and as I dug deeper (with the help of a therapist), I realized that it was because in my childhood, I hadn't felt intrinsic worth by just being me. If I helped someone with their homework at school, that showed I had value. If I helped my mom clip coupons or rubbed my dad's back, I felt useful. The only things I remember being praised for were being smart and obedient. I never received praise for being creative or curious. As a result, I grew up with the belief that doing things for other people was the only way I could demonstrate my worth. No wonder I wanted to be a doctor. I don't know if this is true of everyone who is in an industry that serves others—doctors, teachers, counselors—but I do know it was part of my decision, even if somewhat subconsciously. The problem is that over time, I felt overextended, underappreciated, and burned out from always saying yes.

When you've been a yes-woman all your life, it's the only way you know how to live. Saying no is hard because it's easier to continue doing the same things than to change. But sooner or later, something's got to give. If you keep running at an unsustainable pace, someone or something is going to push you off that treadmill, and you might land hard. You have to remember that *you* control your speed and that *you* control when you get on or off.

It is time to become a different kind of yes-woman—by putting yourself first and by recognizing that the people and things that are most important to you in life will still be there even if you have to say no sometimes. Setting healthy boundaries will help you to feel more in control of your time, space, and energy. This will allow you the bandwidth to decide to whom and to what you want to say yes instead of blindly saying yes to everything and burning out. The goal is not to neglect the people in your life. The goal is to put your oxygen mask on first so that you have the energy and the internal resources to help others. Saying yes is a finite resource, so use it wisely and say it to the people who matter most—including yourself.

JOY PRESCRIPTION

Set Healthy Boundaries for Yourself and Others

- *Prioritize your time.* Ask yourself what needs to be done by you and what can be delegated. What are your priorities? Do the things that absolutely need to be done by you, and stop feeling guilty about outsourcing other things—you can't do it all yourself.
- *Practice learning to say no.* As they say, practice makes perfect. One way I like to say no is "Thank you for thinking of me, but I don't have the bandwidth to take that on." Then take a breath and stop talking. You don't need to offer a reason why. You don't need to explain yourself. Also, remember that "No, thank you" is a complete sentence and perfectly acceptable.
- *Be prepared for backlash.* When you start saying no, it's going to confuse some people. Some may even express dissatisfaction and try to convince you to go back to your old ways. Be firm (but nice) with your boundaries and give others the time to acclimate to the new you. The people who value you for *who you are* and not *what you do* will be supportive.

CHAPTER 7

JOY INTERRUPTED

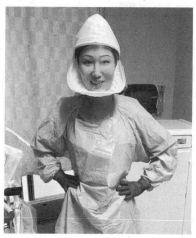

In full PPE during the pandemic

I F YOU ASKED MY FRIENDS TO DESCRIBE ME IN ONE WORD, THEY might say "thoughtful," "responsible," "smart," or "loyal." What they would not say is "spontaneous" or "carefree." I'm not sure if it's my inherent nature, the circumstances of my childhood, or my medical training that makes me a cautious person, but I am what you'd call a "hopeful pessimist." I live my life preparing for the worst and hoping for the best. Somewhere along the way, I adopted this schema to protect myself from disappointment. But I never really thought about how well it was serving me as a life philosophy.

One day I was sitting on the beach (with SPF 50 on and under an umbrella, of course), watching my husband swim with our girls. The sand was warm, the ocean a clear blue, and the weather absolutely perfect.

Wow, this is so nice, I reflected as the sounds of the girls squealing in the water drifted back to me. *I am so lucky.*

Then I started having some intrusive thoughts. First they were little ripples, but then they turned into big waves. Waves that threatened to swallow me.

Life is too good. I'm scared something bad is going to happen.

What if my girls get hurt?

What if something happens to my husband?

What if something happens to me?

As hard as I tried to stay present, my mind went to the dark place I was all too familiar with.

Later, I learned that Dr. Brené Brown calls this feeling "foreboding joy." My first thought upon discovering this was *You mean there's a term for this? It's not just me?* I have since given it my own name: "joy interrupted"—my term for those moments when, in the midst of joy, I flash to a worst-case scenario and worry about how it could all fall apart.

Maybe you've also felt this. Maybe, like me, you've practiced joy interrupted pretty much all your life without being aware of it. When you're an expert in the art of interrupting joy, you know that it's never safe to completely enjoy yourself or relax—because there are so many ways that it could all go wrong.

Joy interrupted started for me at an early age. Because I grew up in an unstable household where my parents constantly fought, we moved every one to two years, and I never felt that I had control over anything—life felt precarious. I never felt happy in the moment because I was always worried that the rug was going to be pulled out from under me. I lived in a constant state of anxiety. Although my parents never actually said this, I knew they felt that if we seemed too happy, too comfortable, too blessed, we'd be tempting the gods. This attitude is actually very common in traditional Chinese culture, in which parents avoid boasting about their children's achievements lest the gods become angry and strike those kids down with a B. That said, my parents did not exactly follow this rule—they were willing to make an exception to brag about my academic successes to their friends, but only with a healthy dose of complaining to go with it. "*Aiya*, Tiffany go to early college program, but we need to pay room and board—it's $8,000—so expensive!" In spite of their constant talk about achievement, I sensed that they were unable to experience true joy in their successes, or mine.

When I gave birth to my daughters, my habit of joy interrupted kicked into full gear. Many parents have stood over the crib, watching their baby sleep—you're not marveling at how cute they are or at the miracle of life. You are watching their chests go up and down to make sure they are still breathing. But for me, becoming a parent meant that my joy interrupted went into overdrive—and all this times two because I had twins. If one of them threw up, I was convinced that she had gastric outlet obstruction and would need surgery. My anxiety was running away with me, and I didn't know how to put on the brakes.

It didn't help that I worked as an anesthesiologist. My profession of choice involves assessing someone's comorbidities and risk for surgery—thinking ahead to everything that could possibly go wrong—and then preemptively doing things to try to mitigate that risk. It is my job to draw up medications that I might never end up using in surgery because if something serious happens, I won't be able to afford those precious extra seconds. Every day I get consent from patients before surgery and inform them that there are certain risks with general anesthesia, including but not limited to dental damage, blood pressure instability, a possible allergic reaction, low oxygen levels, stroke, heart attack, and, yes—even death. It is ingrained in my personality as a doctor to be prepared for the worst. My borderline obsessive habit of joy interrupted made me one hell of an anesthesiologist, but outside the operating room, it was ruining my life.

Added to that, I work at a public county hospital that treats mostly underserved patients. Every day I witness the effects of trauma, from shootings and stabbings to major car accidents. I've learned over the years to leave work at work, but sometimes that's simply impossible. The things I see at work remind me simultaneously of how incredibly lucky I am and of how life can change drastically in a split second. Once, a patient came in who'd stopped his car by the side of the freeway to help someone change a flat tire. In the middle of this selfless act, another car had come by and hit him, dragging him forty feet before stopping. What was lying on the gurney in front of me was almost unrecognizable as a person.

When I got home that day, I said to Daniel, "Don't ever get out of your car by the side of the freeway."

"Why?" he asked.

"Just don't do it. It's dark at night, and other cars can't see you." I knew he was squeamish, and I didn't want to upset him, but at the same time, I couldn't keep the thought out of my head that someday this could happen to him—or someone else I knew.

When I learned that other people also experienced joy interrupted, I thought, *If other people also feel this way, maybe they have a solution to fix this? How can I stop feeling like this? What can I do to start enjoying life in the moment?* In a way, I was comforted to know that I wasn't the only weirdo out there obsessing over bad things that were highly unlikely but could happen in the future. But this feeling of comfort was fleeting because the overachiever in me (basically, my entire personality) immediately went into fix-it mode. Intellectually I knew that I needed to change this habit; otherwise I would never truly be happy. But how was I going to do it?

I read a lot of self-help books. I listened to podcasts. I tried meditation. I tried keeping a gratitude journal. (Gratitude, Brené Brown says, is the key to fully experiencing joy.) Every morning I would write down three things I was grateful for.

Monday: I am grateful for my health, my husband, and my children.

Tuesday: I am grateful for my parents, my job, and the house I live in.

Wednesday: I am grateful for my dogs, my loyal friends, and the eight hours of sleep I got last night.

Thursday: I am grateful for coffee, good Wi-Fi, and Botox.

Friday: I am grateful for Excel spreadsheets, deep-tissue massages, and TSA PreCheck.

Saturday: I am grateful for fresh air, yoga class, and hot Cheetos.

Sunday: I am grateful for my freedom, precut fruit, and laughter.

Have you ever done this? Did it make you more grateful, or was it just another thing you felt like you had to do? Maybe I was doing it all wrong because I only made it a few weeks before it started feeling like another chore. The purpose of the exercise is to pay attention to all the good things we have in our lives instead of taking them for granted. By focusing on the positive aspects of life, according to this journaling practice, we actually rewire our brains to build up resilience against negative situations. That all made sense in theory, but in practice, it wasn't quite working for my brain.

After a while, I shoved the idea of changing my attitude toward joy to the back of my mind. My anxiety served me well, so what was really the problem? Sure, it prevented me from being totally carefree because I was always wondering when the other shoe would drop. But that was just how my brain worked, and it had gotten me pretty far in life. Maybe this was just the way it was for me.

I probably could have gone on this way for quite a long time, with my head in the sand, refusing to address my warped relationship with joy and how it was affecting me and the people around me. But then, in early 2020, the other shoe dropped.

⌢

I HAD SOME EXCITING THINGS PLANNED FOR EARLY 2020.

I was supposed to travel to Europe and South America for medical conferences. My family was planning a trip to Mexico for spring break. We'd just hired an au pair from China who would teach my girls to speak perfect Mandarin so my mom could stop shaming me about that. But then abruptly, because of the global pandemic, my conferences were canceled, spring break was canceled, my kids' school was canceled, and, in effect, life was canceled.

What wasn't canceled, however, was my work at the hospital. There were still cancer patients who needed lifesaving operations and trauma victims who needed emergency surgery. At first I was glad to get out of the house because I needed to do something and to feel useful, and work provided exactly that. But every day there was something new to catastrophize.

A typical day for me during the pandemic went something like this: at 6:30 a.m., I left the house and went out to the garage, where I placed a change of clean clothes in a plastic bin for when I came home from work. Then I drove to the hospital as the sun was coming up. In the parking garage, I scanned my badge to get in as I'd done countless days before. But after that, everything was different. Part of the hospital had been walled off as the COVID unit, and entering that unit was like walking into a scene from *The Twilight Zone*. A sign on the huge double doors said DO NOT CROSS. You had to follow a strict decontamination procedure in which you changed your scrubs, gown, and gloves. The only thing you couldn't change was your mask. In the early days of the pandemic, each hospital employee received one N95 mask that had to last two weeks. If I sneezed inside my mask, all I could do was take it off, wipe out the inside, and put it back on again. Every day when I left work, I prayed, "Please don't let me get sick or bring it home and get anyone else in my family sick."

At 5 p.m., I would get in my car and drive home from the hospital. The first thing I did after pulling into the garage was to decontaminate again, using an outdoor shower that Daniel had installed in the garage a few years earlier. I still remember my conversation with Daniel when we decided to install it:

"Why do we need a bathroom in the garage?" I protested. "Who's going to shower there?"

"It'll be good when our friends come over to swim," Daniel pointed out. "There won't be wet feet coming in when someone needs to use the restroom."

That seemed reasonable to me. The shower never ended up getting much use during poolside entertaining, but throughout the first few months of the pandemic, I used it every day after work. Dubbed "the Decontamination Shower," it was where I would literally and symbolically wash off the day before going inside to see my family. When you do the kind of work that I do, it takes a toll on you—physically, mentally, and emotionally. Particularly during those early days of the pandemic, I just didn't know how to process it or how to leave it behind.

I thought about my girls, who were doing remote kindergarten with our au pair from China during the day. The au pair's English wasn't very strong, so it was hard for her to help them with their homework. At one point, they were supposed to be learning long and short vowel sounds, but she couldn't understand the concept well enough to teach it to them. So, after a long day at work, I'd try to teach my kids to read.

I thought about my parents, whom we hadn't seen in months, even though they lived only three miles away. Since my dad was on immunosuppressants due to his rheumatoid arthritis, they took quarantine very seriously. My mom would even put on a mask and gloves to get the mail, wiping it down before she brought it inside in case the mailman was dropping off some COVID particles.

Alone in the shower, I often cried. I cried for the people we'd lost. I cried for all the people who were struggling to make ends meet. I cried for our community because it felt like everyone was divided and on edge. I cried for my parents, who were afraid to go outside. I cried for myself because I felt so helpless and lost. All my life, I'd gotten through tough situations—moving to America, changing schools every two years, medical school, working as a doctor, raising twins—through sheer determination and hard work. But this situation just couldn't be improved through hard work. My belief in the power of overachieving in order to overcome anything completely fell apart during the pandemic.

I wondered how I had gotten here. I had planned out every moment of my life, worked relentlessly, and surpassed everyone's expectations of me. So why did I feel like an empty shell?

In this moment of crisis, my tactic was to focus on what was important to me. Regardless of what was going on at the hospital, once I got home, I was determined to be there 100 percent as the perfect wife and mom. I programmed myself to not talk about my day. *You're home now. You have to get dinner on the table. Your husband is stressed and needs your support. The kids want you to play with them and be silly.* But that was easier said than done. After spending the day inside doing remote learning, all the girls wanted to do was run around and play. I wanted to spend time with them, but I was utterly drained from work. I just didn't have the energy to go outside with them and be active.

"Let's read a book together or do some coloring," I would tell the girls.

"No, Mama, let's go outside and play tag," Maddie would say.

"Mama's tired, baby, can we just snuggle for a few minutes?" I lay down on the couch, patting the seat next to me.

"But, Mama, you're always tired," Chloe whined.

She was right. And that broke my heart. I was giving the bulk of my physical, mental, and emotional energy to people outside my family so that when I got home, I had hardly anything left to give to the people I loved the most.

After the girls were in bed and I had some time to myself to decompress, I'd scroll through social media and see all the fun things people were doing while they worked from home— or at least it looked that way to me. People were posting about designer loungewear, the best sourdough starter, and finishing their ten-million-piece puzzles. They were all working from home. When I called friends to check on them and ask what they'd done that day, they'd say, "I watched Netflix for six hours while I moved the mouse around so that my computer didn't idle and my boss would think I was working."

Are you kidding me?

I knew I wasn't the only one who felt at odds with the way others were experiencing quarantine. But I started to feel jealous of people who got to stay in their pajamas all day, cuddle with their dogs, and take a nap. I didn't have FOMO (fear of missing out), I had FOMI (fear of missing in).

One evening I was drinking a glass of wine (most of my good ideas come while I'm drinking a glass of wine), and I came up with a brilliant solution that would allow *me* to work from home.

"Babe, I've got a great idea," I said to Daniel. "Sometimes the surgeons use robots to do surgery. Why can't we program the robots to intubate patients, give medications, and put in arterial lines? I could monitor the patient remotely and just tell it what to do."

Daniel thought about it for a moment. "What if the Wi-Fi goes out?" he asked.

Well, that was the end of my Remote Anesthesia System idea.

Since my work-from-home idea wasn't panning out, I started thinking about going part-time. With my kids home from school, I wanted the opportunity to spend more time with them, which working eight to ten hours a day at the hospital didn't offer. Since all in-person conferences were canceled, I signed up for an online health and wellness seminar geared toward female physicians to get my continuing medical education (CME) for the year. One of the speakers had us take the Maslach Burnout Inventory, an assessment that measures occupational burnout. In past conferences, whenever people started talking about burnout, I'd leave the room to use the restroom or get a snack. But now, everything was virtual and I had my camera off, so I just stayed and kept listening. I thought, *There's no way I have burnout.... Isn't that what people use as an excuse when they can't cut it? Not me. I'm fine.*

Well, when I got the results of that test, I was floored. I scored high in each category—emotional exhaustion, depersonalization, and decreased sense of personal accomplishment—and this time, having the highest score wasn't a good thing. The test indicated that I had severe burnout and that some of the irritability and fatigue I was feeling were directly related to it. With this new understanding, I reflected on how I moved through the world. I thought about how my fractured presence, constant anxiety, and frantic hurrying were affecting my husband and children, not to mention my own health.

I tend to be a solution-oriented person, so once I figured out that I had burnout, the next question was *Well, what do I do to fix it?* I distinctly remember using my phone to take a picture of the slide in the presentation that included things like strengthening social connections, setting boundaries, and making sleep a priority. *Right*, I thought, *that all sounds lovely, but how am I supposed to do that when I'm working fifty to sixty hours a week and raising twins?* I knew that something (besides my sanity) had to give.

I knew what I needed to do, but in addition to being afraid to admit to other people that I had burnout, I was even more afraid of asking my boss if I could go part-time. I could just hear his voice: "You want to go part-time? I thought you were a rising star, but I guess you're not." I didn't know of a single part-time faculty member who had a leadership position, ran multiple clinical research trials, or had high academic output. For someone who wanted to climb higher on the academic anesthesiology ladder, asking to go part-time could be, as my mentor had told me years before, career suicide. Also, the timing wasn't exactly great. We were in the middle of a pandemic—how selfish would it be for me to ask to go part-time during this crisis? Maybe I should wait until things got back to normal.

In the meantime, I had other things to focus on. Like many people during the pandemic, I started using social media more to stay connected with others. Not all my interactions were positive, but I always say that your social media is like your house. If someone comes in and is rude and refuses to take off their shoes, they're not invited back. This meant I had no problem blocking people, and there were plenty to block. I couldn't believe some people were saying that COVID wasn't real. Well, it seemed pretty real to me because I spent every day at the hospital, and every morning we'd get an email with a report of how many new COVID cases there were. I was specifically called to intubate several patients in respiratory distress during that time. Previously I had thought that maybe we could all band together and use our collective wisdom, power, and energy to get through this disaster together. But what I saw during this time was a huge and growing divide between people. I began to think that we might never get through it because we couldn't even listen to one another, much less work together toward a common goal. During those dark days, I started to lose my faith in humanity a little.

Through it all, I couldn't help but think that this was the other shoe dropping—for me and for society, in a big way. I had done everything right—setting up the perfect life, acting like the person everyone wanted me to be. But now, "life" as we'd all known it had disappeared. We had no idea when it was coming back. I thought, *If it were to all end here, could I say that I had lived my life to the fullest?* There had been so much joy to take in, yet I'd missed so much of it. Where had my hard work and achievement gotten me if I hadn't learned how to embrace joy? I wondered, *Would I be given another shot? Did I still have time to learn how to live with joy in my life? What kind of example was I setting for my children?*

I thought of my life up to this point as carrying around a bucket. From my childhood, I had started to fill my bucket with the things that I thought would bring me happiness: getting good grades, finishing college and medical school. Then it was making a good paycheck, paying off all my student loans, and getting a house in the right neighborhood. I thought that when the bucket was full, then I would feel whole. But the more I achieved, the more something became apparent.

My bucket had a leak at the bottom.

The more I tried to fill that bucket with awards, distinctions, and the outward signs of success, the more my efforts just seemed to drain out. No wonder I felt empty. Instead of frantically running around trying to fill the bucket, what I needed to do was set my bucket down, fix the leak, and refill it with something more substantial, something that would last—something that would bring me joy. And those things weren't what my parents had chosen for me or what other people expected of me. Unless I was more intentional about what I filled my bucket with, my efforts would continue to leak out. I would continue to feel exhausted and unfulfilled.

Have you been carrying around a leaking bucket too? Are you so exhausted from trying to fill the bucket that you didn't even notice the leak at the bottom? Set it down for a minute and take a breather. What are you filling your bucket with? Is it things that society tells you should make you happy, like material possessions or a high-powered job? Or is it things that feel right for you, that you truly value in life?

After coming to my realization, I decided to live with more intention by choosing things like connection, creativity, gratitude, and laughter instead of climbing the professional ladder and continuing to work for some ideal that could not exist in reality. I chose joy in the present day instead of reaching for some unattainable goal in the far future. I realized there was more to life than achievement and burning myself out to please everyone else. It wasn't an easy realization, and many times it felt uncomfortable—but for me, the process was worth it, and I think it will be for you too.

What do you want to fill your bucket with?

JOY PRESCRIPTION

Live Every Day with Intention

- *Stop trying to dress-rehearse tragedy.* I did this for a long time, which caused me to lose out on precious moments of joy, thinking that it would strengthen my resilience for when something bad happened. But when the other shoe dropped, it didn't do me one ounce of good. Be grateful for the present moment.

- *Practice true gratitude.* Someone told me recently that it can be helpful to think about your problems as blessings, which has really helped me reframe my thinking. When I have to step in because my kids are fighting, I'm grateful that I have two happy, healthy children who are figuring out how to deal with interpersonal conflict. When my muscles are sore from working out at the gym, I'm grateful to be strong and able to exercise. I think of these not as things I *have* to do but as things I *get* to do, which helps put everything in perspective.

- *Consider how you would like other people to remember you.* No one wants to be remembered as the person who never took their vacation days or was the last to leave the office. Instead, they want to be remembered as thoughtful, funny, and generous—in other words, qualities that truly make a difference in other people's lives. How can you take action each and every day to make sure you're remembered for the right reasons?

PART III

CHAPTER 8

GOING OFF SCRIPT

On the set of a *Real Housewives of Dallas*
reunion with Andy Cohen

H AVE YOU EVER DONE SOMETHING COMPLETELY OUT OF CHAR-
acter that you never in a million years would have imagined
yourself doing? Something that blows up your whole life? Something
that makes your friends and family stare at you with open mouths
and ask, "What on earth were you thinking?"

For me, that thing—that unimaginable event—was going on a
reality TV show called *The Real Housewives of Dallas* (*RHOD*).

Some people might have said that I was having a midlife crisis. I was only in my midthirties, but by now you know that I do

everything early. Basically, I was in this existential, *Is this all I'll ever do?* predicament. The kind that can only be resolved by joining the cast of a reality show that you've never seen before, where you know almost no one and have no clue what's going on.

In my midlife rut, I wanted to do something no one expected of me. I felt like I had been a good girl all my life. I had done everything exactly by the book—gone to the right schools, chosen the right career, gotten married, and had kids at the right time. I had never done anything wild and crazy. My credit score was over 800, and I didn't have so much as an unpaid parking ticket (I really sound like the life of the party here, right?). I was a rule follower and Goody Two-shoes, so this was my ultimate act of rebellion.

When I meet people who know that I was on *RHOD*, many of whom have watched me on the show, they have several burning questions. I'll try to answer these questions as openly as I can.

HOW DID YOU GET CAST ON SEASON 5 OF *RHOD*?

I had been friends with one of the cast members, D'Andra Simmons, for years. We were introduced to each other by her mother, whom I affectionately call Momma Dee and whom I'd known from her work with the hospital. I even had a blink-and-you'll-miss-it cameo during D'Andra's birthday party on season 4.

At the end of each season, the producers ask the cast members if they know anyone who would be a good addition to the show. (It's kind of like a sorority—they always need fresh blood.) In 2018, after season 3, D'Andra offered me up. But I had two toddlers and a demanding job, and I didn't yet feel the need to fully rebel against the status quo.

My response when she asked me was "You're joking, right?"

At the conclusion of season 4 in 2019, she asked me again. This time I considered it more seriously. I had recently been promoted from assistant to associate professor at work, and it felt less exciting than I'd thought it would be. I asked myself if I would be happy or satisfied if I kept doing exactly what I was doing every day for the next thirty years, and the answer was no. I felt like something was missing, but I didn't quite know what it was (spoiler alert—it wasn't being on a reality TV show). I called Momma Dee to ask for her advice.

"Dee, I don't know about the show. D'Andra really wants me to do it, but I'm afraid people will judge me."

"Why do you give a rat's ass what other people think?" she said in her signature Southern drawl.

"Well, I'm not as brave as you. I guess there's a part of me that still cares what other people think. What if I do or say something stupid and embarrass myself?"

"Look, I'm almost eighty years old, so I've had more time to realize other people's opinions don't mean anything. Now, I've known you for quite some time, and I'd be shocked if you did anything to embarrass yourself. Just be yourself. Don't you want to show people that you can be a smart, hardworking doctor and still be fashionable and funny?"

"I guess you're right—"

She interrupted before I could finish: "You're damn right I'm right."

The next day I called D'Andra to talk it over with her. She told me that being on the show was a lot of fun. She said that it would be a good opportunity for me to let down my hair and make some new friends. As a selling point, she told me that since I would be the only cast member with a "normal job," production would work around my schedule at the hospital and most of my filming could be done on nights and weekends. I also learned that Bravo paid for the entire cast to go on one local trip (usually over a weekend) and one international trip, which would be closer to one week long. Altogether it would be about twelve weeks of filming. Wait. *Twelve weeks?* That was it? *Well,* I thought, *I can do that.* I had done medical school and a rigorous anesthesiology residency. I had been in a long-distance relationship for three years. I had twins. Surely I could handle *twelve weeks* of filming for a little reality TV show.

"Fine," I told D'Andra. "I'll talk to casting. No promises, though."

The next month I had a Zoom call with the casting director. She asked me some pretty straightforward questions: What did I do for work? Where had I met my husband? What were my kids like? I tried to show myself in the best possible light, but to be honest, I wasn't 100 percent sure that I wanted to do the show. I was aware that some other women in Dallas were also interviewing to be on the show, and many of them *really* wanted the job. Because I felt it was important to be transparent, I told her that I was working full-time with two young kids, and I just didn't know if I would be able to do it, but I was grateful for the opportunity to be interviewed. She seemed understanding and encouraged me to see how the process went.

In January 2020, I went to Los Angeles for a green-screen interview with the executive producer. I sat on a stool with two cameras on me while I answered questions—for three hours straight. Did I know any of the other women on the show? Where did I live, and could I describe my house? How many cars did we own? What kinds of things did my husband and I argue about? What was it like being a full-time physician and a mom to twins? What was my relationship with my mother like? Was it hard growing up as an immigrant in America? How many Birkin bags did I own?

I answered everything truthfully and candidly. A week later, the executive producer, along with a Bravo TV executive, came to my home with a few cameramen to meet my family and film some scene work. This, I learned, was the final stage of "tryouts," in order for them to see how I appeared on camera and how I interacted with others, since the other footage they had was just me sitting and answering questions.

"What should I do to prepare?" I asked the executive producer.

"Nothing," he said. "Just pretend like we're not here and do what you would normally do."

Right, I'll just pretend that there isn't an entire film crew in my house and I don't have a microphone clipped to my dress. Sure, great, easy. Actually though, after the first thirty minutes (and a glass of wine), I started to feel more at ease and not so cognizant of the mic I was wearing, the extra lights they'd set up, and the cameramen in my living room. It went by quickly, and as fast as they'd set up, they were soon breaking down. The producer gave me a hug and said, "We'll be in touch."

Almost a month went by, and I didn't hear anything, so I assumed they'd moved on. Then, on Valentine's Day, I got the call: "Tiffany—we'd like you to join season 5 of *The Real Housewives of Dallas!*"

"Wow, that's great news," I said. "Can I think about it and let you know tomorrow?"

A pause. Clearly this was not the answer he usually got. I think he expected me to squeal or jump up and down with delight, but that's just not my style. Plus, I still didn't know if I wanted to commit to the show.

As with all important decisions in my life, I made a spreadsheet listing the pros and cons of going on *RHOD*. Pros: make new girl-friends, go to cool parties, and travel on an all-expenses-paid vacation courtesy of Bravo TV. (The year before, they had gone to Thailand, one of my favorite countries.) Cons: damage my reputation, make a fool of myself on national television, and piss off my parents.

"What should I do?" I asked Daniel.

"This list is about even," he replied. "At the end of the day, do you want to do it?"

"Part of me wants to, but part of me is scared. I don't know."

"If you don't do it, you'll always wonder what could have been."

Daniel was right. I might never get this chance again, and if I didn't take it, I'd regret not doing it. I'd always lived life so cautiously, doing what other people told me to do, what I thought (they thought) would bring me happiness. Here was an opportunity to do something that *no one* expected from me, that I was choosing for myself.

I called the producer the next day and told him I was in.

DO THEY JUST FOLLOW YOU AROUND WITH CAMERAS 24-7?

No, all the filming is scheduled ahead of time. No one ever shows up at your door unannounced. It's actually quite well organized, and each week you get a "call sheet" that is basically your shooting schedule for that week. On average, you're filming only about two to three days out of the week unless you're on a cast trip. This was one of the hooks they used to convince me that I could handle the filming even while working a full-time job. Every week was a bit different, and everyone's call sheet looked a little different because you might be doing scenes with your family or doing a scene with just one or two other castmates. If I had a particularly heavy schedule at the hospital, they'd cut me some slack and give me some easy family scenes to shoot that week.

The "all-cast" events are bigger and usually scheduled for the weekends. Those were less predictable because when you get that many big personalities in the room, there's bound to be some chaos. Occasionally one of the cameras would have issues or a GoPro would fall off the window it was mounted on, so they'd have to stop filming and fix the equipment. The general rule of thumb for filming is that the more housewives there are, the more cameramen there are (usually one per housewife) and the more mayhem there is. The thing I'd never anticipated that really bothered me was how long it took to film something simple. At my first group event, I had to get out of the car four different times so they could get the shot of the shoe stepping out of the car, then me flipping my hair over my shoulder, then me walking toward the front door, and finally through the front door. It was frustrating, to say the least. They also stagger all the arrivals so that only one or two housewives show up to an event at the same time. You might show up at 7 p.m. but stand around or sit in a car for an hour or two because something is going on and they don't want you walking in and interrupting a moment.

I remember always showing up on time and realizing that many of my castmates treated the start time on their call sheet as more of a suggestion than a requirement. For one event in particular, I worked until 5 p.m., rushed home to shower and change, and showed up at 7 p.m., right when my call sheet said I was supposed to. Some of the other women who also had 7 p.m. call times showed up closer to 8:30. I was furious. I had barely seen my children that day, and now I found that I could have stayed home a little longer with them? I didn't know you could just casually saunter in whenever you felt like it and say something like "Sorry, my glam squad was running behind" or "I had a fashion emergency." (Yes, those were things that were actually stated as reasons for my castmates' tardiness.) Can you

imagine if I showed up to the operating room at 8:30 instead of
7 a.m.? I would be fired so fast. There would go my patient satisfac-
tion scores. I just didn't think it was fair that I was playing by the
rules and following orders when others weren't.

The cameras aren't up 24-7, but when they are, they're everywhere. This is why it baffles me every time a housewife blames her
bad behavior on forgetting that she is being filmed. It's not like there
are hidden cameras in the room and you are being spied on. There is
literally a cameraman with a huge camera on his shoulder following
you around and pivoting when you pivot. Not to mention, there are
also usually extra lights set up, and you've got a microphone clipped
to you. This is why I will never understand (or believe) the "I forgot
I was being filmed" excuse.

IS THE SHOW SCRIPTED?

No, the show is not scripted, *but* it is heavily produced. I was never
handed lines to memorize, but I was heavily encouraged to say
something to another cast member. Whereas in normal life, it
would be rare for me to bring up something that happened last
week, it's a common recipe for the housewives to replay and hash
out any misgivings from previous events. This, in essence, gives
the season and each individual a "storyline" that the audience can
follow.

Even though the show isn't scripted, the producers definitely like
to give you some direction on what they'd like you to discuss. Sometimes they would even feed you a line or phrase to prime you to
have it in your head so that you were more likely to say it (some
housewives were more susceptible to these suggestions than others).
It could take six hours to film a dinner scene that would end up
being edited down to twenty minutes of TV airtime. Because the

cast members would arrive at different times, it could take two to three hours to bring everyone to the table. By that point, we were all hungry, restless, and on edge.

Let me tell you, being pushed into a pool by a drunken cast member with all my clothes on and in full hair and makeup was *not* in the script. (Yes, this happened.) Thank goodness I wasn't holding a Birkin at the time. That day I had gone to work and rushed home to meet my glam team. We'd been told to wear all white for a fellow cast member's birthday party, so I had bought a brand-new white jumpsuit. During the party, I was telling the birthday girl that I was stressed out from work and wanted to loosen up and have some fun. The next thing I knew, I was having tequila poured into my mouth straight from the bottle and then being pushed into the swimming pool. The pool wasn't that deep—my toes could touch the bottom—but my clothes and hair and makeup were ruined. Some of the other women laughed. I felt like I was being hazed.

Another unscripted but produced moment was when the producers encouraged me to confront another cast member about a video she had made months earlier mocking the shape of her own eyes. I didn't think she'd meant to hurt anybody with it, but the producers kept asking me how I *really* felt about the incident. Finally I told them what I thought they wanted to hear—that it was insensitive and could be triggering to some people. They continued to tell me to confront her, even after I'd repeatedly told them I'd rather not. Finally, when backed into a corner, I did what they told me to do. I told her that I thought her video was crude and that when I was little, other kids made fun of the shape of my eyes. Afterward, when I was on my way to the bathroom, one of the junior producers caught my eye, mouthed, "Good job," and gave me a thumbs-up. I was just relieved to be done with my assignment.

WHO PAYS FOR THE EVENTS AND
TRIPS ON THE SHOW?

While the show pays for the cast trips, the cast members pay for the events they each host throughout the season, such as dinners and birthday parties. The thinking is that you would have these events even if the show wasn't being filmed, so there's no reason why Bravo should pay for them. Everyone knows that's not exactly true and that the parties become amplified once you know there will be cameras rolling. I didn't want to do all that—I wanted to show my life exactly as I actually lived it. The two events I hosted were a dim sum brunch at a local restaurant and a pizza party in my backyard—very low-key compared to a typical Real Housewife event.

Additionally, aside from the confessionals (a cutaway where a cast member speaks directly to the camera), you are responsible for doing or paying for your own hair and makeup. A friend advised me to hire a "glam squad" for the all-cast events because they were guaranteed to be shown. "Really?" I asked her. "Is that really necessary?" Previously I'd had my hair and makeup done for my wedding, maternity photo shoot, and a few big charity events. Nonetheless, I followed her advice and booked my hair and makeup team for every all-cast event. So even while I was crying, complaining, or fighting, at least my makeup and hair were on point.

What is always free, however, is the alcohol...and the showrunners make sure it is abundantly available. Before shooting starts, you're asked what your favorite drink is (tequila, vodka, red wine, champagne, etc.), and that drink is always at your side. I mean, I'm not one to complain about free alcohol, but I just wished it came with some food. In retrospect, I think the fact that dinner took four hours to be served but alcohol flowed freely was a strategic move to loosen up the cast, if you know what I mean.

WHO CAME UP WITH YOUR TAGLINE: "I CAN SAVE YOUR LIFE BUT NOT YOUR REPUTATION"?

Before I joined *RHOD*, I had no idea that your tagline was such a big deal. When I told my friends I was doing the show, they'd ask, "What's your tagline?" And the answer was "I don't know" because the taglines are actually filmed at the end of the season. Based on what happens during the season, the producers give you four or five potential taglines. Then you sit next to a microphone and say each of them, emphasizing different words each time. For example, I would say, "*I* can save your life but not your reputation." Then I would say, "I can save your *life* but not your *reputation*."

I don't remember what the other ones I read were, but I do remember a few that Daniel and I came up with that we thought they could use. Daniel's favorite was "I'm just like Doogie Howser, except I'm real." I came up with "I put people to sleep for a living, but I'm here to wake you up." The producers were gracious enough to pretend they thought these were good and let me read them for the microphone. Obviously they weren't chosen.

You don't know which one they've chosen until the first episode comes out. When I first heard my tagline, I was disappointed that they hadn't chosen the one I'd come up with, but in retrospect, I think the one they chose perfectly summed up my season on the show. Go ahead, think of some for yourself. If you were to write a tagline for yourself and your life, what would it be?

WHAT WAS WITH THE CHICKEN-FOOT INCIDENT?

When it was time to host my first event, I thought I would take the women to do one of my favorite activities: eat—dim sum, to be exact. My family and I have dim sum at least once a month, and this particular restaurant had a special place in my heart—it was where

Daniel and I had taken my parents to tell them that I was pregnant with twins. As the producers and I were going over the plan, they asked what I normally order at dim sum.

"Oh, the regular things—like shrimp dumplings, shumai, barbecue pork buns, and chicken feet."

That seemed to catch their attention. "Did you just say chicken feet?"

"Yeah, it's a traditional dim sum dish—it's delicious, my kids love it."

"You have to make sure that everyone tries a chicken foot."

"Ahhh, okay. Sure, that's a good idea." I obviously had no idea this was going to become *a thing*.

Now, I'll admit that chicken feet may not sound very appetizing, but have you ever tried them? They're braised until they're soft, and they're a great source of collagen. They are sweet and savory, and everyone I've introduced them to says they're quite tasty (once you get over the idea that you have a foot in your mouth). But of course, at dim sum on *RHOD*, one of the cast members made a big deal out of it, pretending to gag and refusing to try it. At first I was fine with the fact that she wasn't into the chicken feet (fine, more for me). But my producer was adamant that I make her try it. Exasperated, I did what I was told and tried to make a moment. "Just try a damn piece of foot," I insisted.

In hindsight, I shouldn't have been so pushy about trying to convince someone to eat something she didn't want to eat. In real life, I would never act like that. But then again, we were filming for a reality TV show, and no one is going to tune in to watch us sitting around drinking tea and exchanging niceties. My castmate who refused the foot knew that we were filming a TV show, and she saw the producer literally prodding me to make her try one. When we left the restaurant, I thought we were in a good place and that any talk of chicken feet was over, but boy, was I wrong. Many more conversations followed, which became even worse off-screen (more on this later). I eventually dubbed this episode and its aftermath "Chicken Feet Gate."

IS THERE ANYTHING YOU WISH YOU HAD DONE DIFFERENTLY ON THE SHOW?

Between agreeing to join the show and when filming began, I watched the entire previous season of *RHOD* as "homework." I wrote down in my notebook that the cast liked to play practical jokes and pranks on one another but that these pranks were mostly harmless and not that deep. I'd never had siblings to play pranks on because Josh had been born when I was eleven, and I was looking forward to participating in some good old-fashioned juvenile fun with the women. So I decided to play a little practical joke that involved using crickets as a pizza topping at the party that I hosted at my house.

I know that sounds gross, but in my defense, they were FDA-approved crickets that came in a package with nutritional facts on the back that I ordered off Amazon. It's not like I just went into my backyard and foraged for wild crickets and fried them up with some seasoning. I'd seen an episode of *Shark Tank* in which Mark Cuban made a deal with a guy who makes protein bars out of cricket flour. I was just trying to expand the women's culinary palates. I imagined that they would respond with a few *ewww*s and *oh my gosh*es, and then we'd laugh about it. In the future we would start sentences with "Do you guys remember that time with the crickets?" and then take a sip of wine and laugh. That was how I thought it would all go down.

Well, if you've seen the episode, you know that's not what happened. After I told the women that there were crickets on the pizza they'd just eaten, one of them became physically ill and had to run to the bathroom. I regret that my practical joke made her sick. I felt terrible about it and apologized profusely, but there was nothing I could do to take it back. When that episode aired and I watched it, it was all very cringey. I kept thinking, *Why the hell was I trying so hard?*

I was bending over backward to fit in with the rest of the cast and do what I thought the producers expected of me. Looking back, I wish I had relaxed more and just gone along for the ride. But that is easier said than done when you've got cameras in your face, producers who keep telling you to make a moment, and castmates trying to pick a fight over the stupidest things.

DID ANYTHING GOOD COME OUT OF BEING ON THE SHOW?

Yes, but not in the way you would think. I didn't launch a business that I promoted on the show and later sold for millions of dollars. I didn't make many new friends from the show. I didn't go to any fancy parties or vacations. But *RHOD* helped me figure out my work-life balance because it gave me the kick in the butt I needed to finally go part-time at the hospital. It was something I'd been thinking about for years, and it had been even more on my mind since the pandemic had started, but it never felt like the right time. It was also one of the issues that the producers of the show made specifically mine—they presented me as the cast member with the work-life balance problem (since I was one of the only cast members who worked outside the home). They filmed me talking about it with my husband, and in doing so, I gained some clarity about what decision I should make. This clarity gave me the final push to schedule a meeting with my boss to request a change to work part-time.

The week leading up to the meeting, I practiced what I was going to say. I wrote down all the things I had done for the department in the eight years I'd been there. Then I thought of possible rebuttals my boss might make and prepared responses to them. I'm not great at dealing with conflict in the heat of the moment, but if I practice what I need to say, I do much better. I knew this from past experiences when, in the moment, I hadn't stood up for myself. Then later, I'd think of a bunch of things I could have said, beating myself up for not saying them during the conversation.

The day finally came, and I walked over to my boss's office. We started with some small talk, and then I said, "Out of respect for your time, sir, I won't beat around the bush. I've come to ask your permission to go part-time so that I can focus on some other endeavors outside of medicine and spend more time with my family."

I went on with my prepared list of all the contributions I'd made to the department and how dedicated I was to my job. I assured him that this wasn't just me trying to have a slow exit from medicine.

He listened intently and then said, "What do you want?"

"I want to go down to 80 percent."

"Okay. Let's change it on your contract for next year."

And that was that. It was simple. He said yes so quickly that I didn't even need to bring up any of the counterarguments I'd prepared. I kicked myself for not asking sooner. If it hadn't been for *RHOD*, I probably would have soldiered on in silent exhaustion, but the conversations I'd had on the show about work-life balance had pushed me to actually go after what I wanted. For that, I'll always be grateful.

DO YOU EVER REGRET DOING THE SHOW?

This is the question I'm asked the most. And the truth is that it's complicated. While I was filming, especially in the first few weeks, there were definitely moments when I regretted having agreed to be on the show. The truth is that I don't regret it, but I wish I could have had a different cast. (As you know, that's not the way it works.)

The first two weeks of shooting were hard—much harder than I'd anticipated. I went in expecting to make new friends, but instead, I felt like I had walked onto the set of *Mean Girls*. The other cast members all knew one another, and I was the new girl at the playground. *Not this again*, I thought, recalling those elementary school days. The mean-girl behavior—including calling me boring, encouraging me to drink more than I wanted to, and mocking me for having a curfew—was so relentless that after week two, I asked the producers if I could be demoted to "friend of," which means that you are more of a part-time cast member and don't have to attend all the events, like the cast trips. I wanted off that roller coaster. But once you're strapped in and the bar comes down, you can't get off until the end. I was told absolutely not, I had to stick it out. Every week I would say to Daniel, "Three weeks down, nine more to go," and then "Four weeks down, eight more to go," and so on. I was relieved when we went to Southfork Ranch to film the finale because the finish line was in sight.

I don't mean to say that the experience was *all* bad. There were also some good moments. While we didn't get to take a cast trip to an exotic location because of the pandemic, our cast trip to Oklahoma was actually fun, especially after the cameras went down and we continued to hang out into the wee hours of the morning. I did my first-ever beer bong on that trip, gagging and laughing at the same time, beer coming out of my nostrils. And I actually peed myself a little because we were all laughing so hard when one of my castmates, dressed in a Bigfoot costume, surprised us at dinner. (I have a weak pelvic floor from having had twins and all.) One of the other cast members also threw me a birthday party, which made me feel closer to the other women. I felt like that party was a pivotal moment when I started to feel more comfortable on the show and not afraid to show my true personality.

By the last month of shooting, I had hit my stride, and it seemed like my conflicts with my castmates had mostly resolved themselves. I started to feel like we were finally becoming friends. Unfortunately, that feeling evaporated when the show aired a few months later and I tuned in to see these women saying mean things about me behind my back. For instance, some of my castmates came over to my house to catch up, and afterward, I took them to my closet to show them a new custom bag I'd gotten. When the show aired, I was surprised to hear one of my castmates saying that it seemed like I was show-ing off and calling me "tacky." *Wow,* I thought, *that's not what you said at the time.* The amount of two-faced behavior was unreal. Even though the show had been filmed months before, and the conflicts being discussed were in the past, it was hurtful to watch. Most of all, I was embarrassed that I'd started to think these women were actu-ally my friends. As I watched the show, it became very clear to me that they were not. It felt like picking open an old wound that was almost healed and then pouring salt on it.

About two-thirds of the way into the season airing, you have to start getting ready to go to New York City to film the reunion. The week before you travel, the network sends you all the remaining epi-sodes of the show—generally four or five—so you get an idea of how the season ends for everyone. In essence, you get to see the next month's worth of episodes early. For anyone who is unfamiliar with the reunion show, it's the season finale, with Andy Cohen serving as the host and referee. Everyone sits onstage in full glam, and each woman gets her turn in the "hot seat" as her key moments from the season—the good, the bad, and the ugly—are aired.

Prior to doing the show, I didn't know how big a deal the seating arrangement of the reunion was. I later learned that your proximity to Andy is a reflection of how well you did that season. It turned out that my seat was right next to Andy. As I walked onto the stage in my custom Esé Azénabor beaded dress, I cursed myself for not taking the shot of tequila that D'Andra had offered me in my dressing room. I had wanted to have my full faculties going into the ring, but now I was feeling super nervous and jittery. While the rest of the cast was seated, Andy went through the note cards in his hands containing various questions that had been sent in by viewers, which we'd have to answer. We weren't given any of the questions in advance, but I think most of us had an inkling of what we were going to be asked about.

If a question is about a conflict between two cast members, each person is given the chance to speak, going back and forth until some sort of resolution is reached and Andy moves on to the next question. Our reunion aired as two forty-three-minute episodes, but filming took all day. I got into hair and makeup at 7 a.m., and we didn't wrap filming until around 10 p.m., at which time everyone was beyond exhausted. My back hurt from sitting up straight for so long, my brain hurt from having to argue all day, and the beads from my dress had made indentations in my butt. I wanted nothing more than to go back to my hotel room to wash off my makeup and slip into my pajamas. My blood pressure was so high that I ended up having a nosebleed. D'Andra assured me, "There's no way they'll air that," but a few weeks later, my final moments on Bravo TV showed me having a nosebleed, again trying too hard to "make a moment."

The reunion is framed as an opportunity to hash out misgivings and discuss any unresolved conflicts from the season. I thought it might be a chance for me to get some closure on everything that had happened. I went in with a clear head and high hopes, but those hopes quickly faded when one of my castmates brought up a spat we'd had on social media, where she'd said she'd rather eat one of her dog treats than chicken feet. Yes, we were back to Chicken Feet Gate again. She had seen some of my social media posts where I put on a wig and pretended to be my mother, acting out scenes from my childhood. She reasoned that this was stereotyping and that "stereotyping was racism"; therefore, I was racist. *Huh? So I'm racist? Against my own race? Because I made fun of my own mother?* My brain hurt.

This was particularly ironic because the one relationship in my life that was unexpectedly strengthened by my being on the show was my relationship with my mom. Even before shooting started, I suspected that the producers were going to focus on my relationship with my mom (Mama Drama, as I like to call it). During my casting interviews, I had been pretty open in describing my relationship with my mom and all the things she had done that irked me, like throwing a house slipper at me when I hadn't made a perfect SAT score, telling me I was too skinny one week and then too fat the next, or criticizing how I was raising my kids. "It's complicated, like the relationship status on Facebook," I said when they asked me about my relationship with my mother. "I love my mother very much—if she needed a kidney, I would give one to her in a heartbeat—but she drives me crazy on a day-to-day basis."

My intention was never to have my parents on the show—in fact, I didn't even tell them I was doing it. But as things progressed, the producers kept urging me to talk to my mom on-screen about our ongoing issues. I refused at first, but week after week they kept bringing it up until I finally gave in. The timing was perfect because her birthday and my girls' birthday are five days apart and were coming up soon. I decided that I would disguise my need for her to come film with me as a request from my daughters to see their "Grammy" for their birthday (they had been saying they missed her).

I called her and said, "Mom, can you come over and make your homemade dumplings next week? The girls really miss you and want to see you for your birthday. They painted some pictures they wanted to give you." All true.

My mom may be able to say no to me, but she has a hard time when it comes to her granddaughters. "Of course I can come," she said.

"Oh, by the way, I'm filming for a little TV show, so you'll need to wear a small microphone, and there will be a cameraman filming us. But he won't ask you any questions, so you don't have to talk to him. Just ignore him and pretend he's not there. Okay? Can't wait to see you—byeeee!" I hung up before she had time to question me.

A few days later, my mom came over to my house to make dumplings. (She makes the best dumplings from scratch.) I was feeling guilty for tricking her into coming over and filming when she thought she was just coming over to see her granddaughters and have a nice dinner. We made small talk while I deliberately tried to avoid looking in the direction of my producer, who I knew was motioning for me to talk to her. When the dumplings were almost ready, my mom said she wasn't going to eat with us because she needed to go back home to make dinner for my dad. Normally I wouldn't have pressured her to stay, but I knew that if I didn't talk to her like my producer wanted, I was going to get in trouble. So I asked my mom if she could stay for just a little while and eat a few dumplings with us while they were hot.

As we ate, we got to talking about how when I first came to America at six years old, she frequently took me to the library because she was busy studying. During these trips, she'd pack us leftovers for lunch, and we'd eat outside, sitting on the steps of the library. I'd purposely drop some rice so I could watch the pigeons come over and peck at the grains. Occasionally she'd hand me a dollar and tell me I could get a snack from the vending machine. She even brought a blanket with her so I could take a nap at her feet under the cubicle while she studied.

"I feel like because you were working so hard during that time, we missed out on so much," I said to her. "You were so busy."

"But we still hang out," my mom responded. "Every weekend we hang out together. Sometimes we take a walk. We have the flashing card…"

"We had flash cards, that's true," I acknowledged. I had an instant flashback to the thick pack of vocabulary flash cards my mom used to quiz me on. I would say the word out loud and then say the definition. If I got it right, it went into one pile, and if I got it wrong, it went in another pile. We just kept going until everything was in the correct pile.

Then I pointed out how I'd left the house at fifteen years old to go to the early college entrance program. "Moving out of the house when you're fifteen is not normal, Mom," I said.

"It's normal for kids who get selected. It's a good thing," she replied.

"My academic advancement was a good thing. But I think it came at the expense of mother-daughter time. I feel like we missed out on a lot of opportunities to be together." Years of resentment and sadness came tumbling out. "I always just feel like no matter what I do, I'm letting you down. You're never happy with me. I'm always messing something up."

"Who said that?"

"*You* said that. You're always picking on me."

As I started to cry, my mom pulled me into her arms for a hug. Then she said the words I had waited to hear for so long: "I love you."

"I'm sorry, I don't want to disappoint you anymore," I said through my tears.

At this point, my mom was crying too. "You never disappoint me. You're my love, my pride. I only have one daughter, so don't ever say that, okay?"

"I just want you to be proud of me."

"I'm very proud of you."

My mom had never said that to me before. Even though I knew deep down that she loved me, it was different to hear her say those words out loud. Growing up, I'd always longed to hear them, and now she was saying them, unbidden, thanks to a TV show. Trust me, the irony is not lost on me. Because of *RHOD*, those moments are preserved on film for eternity. I'll never need to wonder if I imagined it because I can just rewatch it on TV. It was a *forced* moment, but it was a *true* moment. Even though the reason for us coming together was contrived, the emotions were genuine, and my mom ended up saying words that I will always remember.

I love you. I'm very proud of you.

This conversation with my mom was very eye-opening for me. The more I thought about it, the more I came to realize that this feeling I'd had that my mom had not been proud of me was just that—a feeling. I had spent years telling myself that nothing I did was good enough for my mom and that she would never be proud of me—even though this was not the truth of how *she* felt. Why had I adopted this false narrative of my mom never having been proud of me? As I have come to understand it, I must have developed it to deal with my own fear of never feeling like I was good enough or worthy. Perhaps, I reasoned, if I wasn't even good enough for my own mother to love me and be proud of me, I needed to keep working harder and achieve more until I was worthy.

Sometimes we make up stories about ourselves that become an integral part of our identity, and we use these stories to explain why we feel a certain way. These false narratives might help us cope in the moment, but ultimately they limit us and can become cages. And if these narratives are based on assumptions about other people that turn out not to be true, they can also harm our relationships and keep us from moving forward with those people, and with ourselves.

Because for so long I felt that my mom wasn't proud of me, I saw every interaction between us through a lens of disappointment. Everything I did was colored by the uncertainty of whether my mom would praise me or reprimand me. I was still that little girl who felt worthless, who longed for her approval. But when I let go of that idea—when I realized it was all in my head—I was able to appreciate my mom for the sacrifices she'd made, and our relationship became stronger for it.

So when people ask me whether doing *RHOD* was worth it, I say yes—I learned so much and it was an eye-opening experience. It gave me the fortitude to finally ask to go part-time at work. But what I'm most grateful for is that it pushed me to confront a false narrative so that I could move on and rebuild my relationship with my mom. It helped me form the kind of narrative that I want—a true narrative that's based on shared memories, love, and respect. While years of conflict haven't magically been erased, my mom and I understand each other better now and feel closer to each other.

Sure, becoming a Real Housewife was going off script for me, but it rewarded me in the most unexpected ways.

JOY PRESCRIPTION

Take a Leap of Faith

- *Don't say no immediately.* If someone offers you the chance to do something outside your comfort zone and your first instinct is to say no, think about why that is. Could it be that you have a limiting belief that's holding you back? Take some time to go through all the positives and the negatives before making your final decision. The primitive part of our brain wants to keep us safe, and generally anything seen as new is marked unsafe. But realize that comfort and growth cannot exist simultaneously, so sometimes you need to get uncomfortable in order to grow.

- *Consider that what you may gain from the experience may be very different than what you went into the experience hoping for.* I thought I was going on a show to make new friends, go on an awesome trip, and be more lighthearted and fun, but instead, the experience forced me to confront issues with my work-life balance and relationship with my mother. Even if the experience may not end up the way you want it to, you may gain valuable insights or strengthen connections in your life. Sometimes the reward can be the lessons learned from the experience rather than the experience itself.

- *Think about whether you will always be asking yourself, "What if?"* Ten years from now, if you look back on this opportunity that you turned down, will you feel that you missed out on something that could have had an impact on your life? Will you regret not doing something more than doing it? Sometimes you just have to take a leap of faith.

CHAPTER 9

FINDING MY VOICE

Standing proud

WHEN PEOPLE CALL ME AN INFLUENCER, I CRINGE A LITTLE. My intention was never to influence people when I first started building a community on social media. I just wanted to share the things I liked and connect with others as an outlet for my stress and loneliness. In many ways, social media was a form of escapism for me—escape from the hospital, toddler tantrums, and not having much creativity or laughter in my life. I enjoyed watching others' fashion, travel, and beauty content. But like many aspects of my life, my relationship with social media evolved into something beyond what I had originally anticipated.

Maintaining a balanced, healthy relationship with social media has definitely been a learning process for me. One of the most important things I have learned is that *how* you choose to use social media will determine *what* you get out of it. As they say, technology is a great servant but a poor master. If you check your phone dozens of times a day, obsess over your follower count, and mindlessly scroll through your feed, you may be letting social media control you. If you use social media to keep in touch with people, learn new things, and relieve some stress, you're using the tool to your advantage. You need to set boundaries or else the servant will quickly become the master.

Some people think that I only became well-known on social media because of *Real Housewives*. And while *RHOD* certainly increased my following, by the time the show aired, I already had hundreds of thousands of followers. The way I got my start on social media was kind of an accident. At the start of the pandemic, my stepdaughter, Nicole, who was fifteen at the time, encouraged me to do dance challenges with her on TikTok. Because we were all stuck at home together, the whole family got in on it, and it became a stress-relieving and bonding experience for all of us. I remember times when we laughed hysterically while dancing together. There was one glow-stick dance challenge that my kids thought was particularly hilarious. We also did a Fruit by the Foot challenge to see who could eat theirs first without using any hands. Even our dogs participated in some of the challenges. To this day, those memories are etched into my brain and make me smile whenever I think of them.

Eventually I started making my own videos in which I modeled "quarantine fashion," shared my skincare routine, and performed skits imitating my Chinese mother. To my surprise, people responded to them, and little by little, my following started to grow. At work, I had to maintain a certain demeanor as an anesthesiologist, clinical researcher, and professor, but on social media, I wasn't afraid to just be myself and be silly. After all, I was doing it on my own time away from work, and I felt a sense of freedom to do what I wanted and not be constrained by any rules.

When I made the decision to start posting content on social media, I knew that I would receive feedback, both positive and negative. I just didn't expect the level of public scrutiny that comes with putting yourself out there. My followers noticed *everything*, and *all of it* was up for commentary. Well, as they say, opinions are like assholes—everyone has one. For example, at one point, one of the stones on my wedding ring came loose, and I didn't wear the ring for a while because it was at the jeweler being fixed. The next thing I knew, sharp-eyed viewers had spotted my empty ring finger and were speculating about whether my marriage was on the rocks. Another time, some followers asked why I was always talking about fashion and beauty but never medicine and questioned whether I was even a "real doctor."

At the height of the airing of *RHOD*, I was receiving hundreds of comments and direct messages (DMs) a day. Some of them made me feel proud and good inside:

> *I've never watched* Real Housewives *before, but I'm watching because of you.*
> *This show makes me realize how important Asian representation is.*
> *I love that you're a practicing physician and a mom, but that you also love fashion and have a sense of humor.*

And others just made me want to crawl into bed and cry:

> *I'd like to see you choke on a chicken foot.*
> *Put those shoe covers over your chinky eyes and go back to*
> *China bitch.*
> *Why do you think your this important doctor when all you do*
> *is put people to sleep?* (I should have known better than to
> pay attention to someone who didn't know the difference
> between *you're* and *your.*)

The racist comments I immediately reported, and the just plain
mean ones I blocked, but it was hard for me to let some of it go.
It was especially difficult because I'm a people pleaser—I've always
wanted other people to like me—and sometimes I felt gravely mis-
understood. The trouble was that I hadn't yet learned what to pay
attention to and what to dismiss. I confided in a friend who was a
physician and big on social media that I didn't know how to deal
with some of the mean comments I was getting.

"Here's the thing, Tiffany," she said. "If you wouldn't let them
into your *house*, don't let them into your *head*."

I repeated that to myself and nodded—it seemed to make sense.
But I guess I must have look confused because she kept going:
"Okay, let me put it like this. If there's someone at your door trying
to come in, what's the first thing you want to know about them?"

Quickly I answered, "Can they take their shoes off?"

"No, silly, you want to know *who this person is.*"

Back then I was letting everyone into my head without even
knowing who they were or what they wanted. Needless to say, this
was doing terrible things to my mental health.

The kind of mean comments I got were primarily about three
things:

1. How my voice was annoying or my face was ugly.
2. How what I was wearing was inappropriate or unattractive.
3. How "unprofessional" it was for me to be dancing, talking about shoes and purses, and making funny skits.

The first one about my voice hit me particularly hard because I've always been insecure about the way I sound. When I was learning English at the age of six, my goal was to one day speak English so well that everyone would think I was a native English speaker. If I called you and you picked up the phone, you wouldn't think a little Chinese girl was on the other end. Well, I definitely achieved that goal, because now everyone tells me I sound like I'm from the Valley.

While I was growing up, my parents emphasized the importance of speaking proper American English. "You must always speak perfectly and use your words correctly," my dad would say to me. I thought they were just being hard on me, but now I realize they were trying to protect me because they didn't want me to experience the racism and discrimination they faced. I often saw them being treated differently because they had thick accents and frequently used incorrect words. Once, while in the car, we were rear-ended. When my dad tried to explain what had happened, I remember the police officer making fun of him: "Light is red, so she should no going, but she going?" Even as a child, I understood the mockery and condescension in his voice.

As a teenager, I'd often be my parents' spokesperson on the phone so that whoever was on the other end of the line would treat us fairly. I remember whenever my mom needed to make important phone calls to companies, she would tell me what to say, and I would translate for her. I felt really useful in this way and always felt a pang of pride when my mom said, "Tiffany-ah, come over here. I need your help to make a phone call."

I distinctly remember the first time I was aware of what my voice sounded like. When I was thirteen years old, I left a message on a friend's answering machine (remember those?). Later, when we were at her house, she was checking the messages to see if her mom had called, but instead my voice came out: "Hi, Sarah, it's Tiffany. I'm just making sure you want me to come over after school; my mom says she's gonna drop me off at four." This was the first time I'd heard my voice, and I was appalled.

"Do I really sound like that? Is there something wrong with your answering machine?" I asked my friend.

"No, the answering machine is fine," she assured me. "That's just how you sound."

Years later, when I was asked to give lectures at the hospital and present my research at national medical conferences, I hired a speaking coach to work with me. She instructed me on how to improve my inflection, tone, and cadence, but what I really wanted was for her to teach me to sound less annoying.

"Can I ask you a question?" I asked her. "Does my voice sound annoying to you?"

"No, not particularly," she answered. "What bothers you about your voice?"

"It's just so nasal. Like when I hear myself, it sounds like I'm pinching my nose while I'm talking."

She chuckled. "Your voice sounds just fine. I wouldn't worry about it. You're not Fran Drescher."

But was I? Fast-forward several years. If you think listening to yourself on an answering machine is bad, try watching yourself for forty-five minutes every week for eighteen weeks on TV. Every time my mouth opened on-screen, I winced at the sound that came out of it. Then came the predictable comments:

Your voice is so annoying.
Why do you talk like that?
Why are you trying to sound like a Kardashian? What's wrong
with you?

Believe me, I know my voice is annoying. I've tried to do something about it, but I can't change the way I sound. Some people don't like their nose; I don't like my voice. But until voice transplants are a thing, I'll just have to deal with it.

Likewise, the second-most-popular type of comment—about what I was wearing—was about something I could, but wouldn't, change. These comments tended go something like this:

I can't believe you left the house in that.
You shouldn't wear that, you're a mom.
Aren't you a little too old to be baring your midriff?

That last one is usually said by a man—or at least someone I'm assuming is a man, since a lot of the commenters won't show their faces or use their real names.

Another thing I've learned about social media is that people say things in your comments or DMs that they would *never* say to you in person (if they even had the opportunity to speak to you in person). The worst offenders don't have their own picture or name associated with their account—I call these people "trolls" or "keyboard warriors." Meanwhile, everything I post is under my name, which means I have to take responsibility for the things I say. I have to admit, I've responded to trolls more often than I should—usually after having a glass or two of wine. But I firmly believe in the old adage: "Never wrestle with pigs. You both get dirty, and the pig likes it." Sometimes I think that trolls say outrageous or triggering things on purpose to get your attention so that you will respond to them, but don't fall for this. These people are toxic, and there's no use in trying to engage them—block and move on.

Finally there are the comments about how my interest in fashion, dancing, beauty, and luxury goods undermines my credibility as a physician:

> *You're so unprofessional. I would never want you as my doctor.*
> *You must not take your job that seriously if you have time to make TikToks.*
> *All you ever do is talk about purses and shoes. You're so superficial.*

As my friend suggested, I had to stop and think about *who* was saying these things. If someone you knew and whose opinion you valued was trying to tell you something, of course you'd listen to them. But if a stranger on the street yelled something at you as you walked by, you'd probably just ignore them and go about your day. That's the weird thing about social media—even though in real life, you'd ignore this person, sometimes you let someone whom you'd *never* let into your house get into your head.

One day Daniel came home and found me sulking on the sofa.

"Babe, what's wrong?" he asked.

"Someone said that I was unprofessional and they were going to report me to the medical board!" I said, showing him the comment.

"Report you for what? Having a glass of wine and dancing in your pajamas? This person has no profile picture and four followers," he pointed out. "Why do you even care what they think?"

Why *did* I care? Was this about me or about them? I started to wonder about the kind of person who leaves these kinds of comments. Maybe they don't have a good mindset. Maybe they're going through a difficult time. Maybe they're a miserable person, and it makes them feel better to dump on someone else. *Hurt people hurt people*—I'd heard that before, but now it started to make more sense. The more I thought about it, the more I ended up feeling sorry for them, because these kinds of comments indicate way more about the person leaving them than about the person they're directed to.

⌒

ON *RHOD*, WHILE THE EPISODES ARE AIRING, YOU'RE EXPECTED as a cast member to post on social media about that week's episode to try to boost viewership and engagement. When the chicken-foot incident happened in episode 2, one of my castmates, to promote her dog-food line, posted that she'd rather eat dog food than a chicken foot.

This was about six months after the actual incident had happened in real life, and I'd pretty much forgotten about it. But when I saw that, I had an instant, visceral reaction. Suddenly I was transported back to my childhood, when I would bring my lunch to school. My mom would pack rice with meat and vegetables and chopsticks to eat it with, but because it wasn't a ham-and-cheese sandwich or PB&J, my classmates would say, "Ewww, nasty; what *is* that?"

That feeling of shame burned as brightly for me now as it had back then. Also, there's the connotation that Chinese people eat disgusting foods and are less than human because of it. During the pandemic, several people asked me on social media if I served bat at my home. What many of us don't realize is that the foods we think of as appropriate to eat are wholly dependent on culture and familiarity. What sounds disgusting to you might be completely normal for another person, and that should be respected. There's a saying some people teach to children: "Don't yuck my yum." If children can understand and abide by that, I certainly thought a middle-aged "socialite" would too. The old Tiffany would probably have ignored the dog-food/chicken-foot post, but this time was different. I'd spent my whole life enduring comments like this and saying nothing. But now I felt like I had finally found my voice, and I didn't want to be silent and "let it go."

I had to respond to that post. What ensued was basically a social media war in which insults were volleyed back and forth. It was certainly not my finest moment, but I was coming from a place of hurt and reactiveness. The most ridiculous thing about it all was that this conflict was about something that had happened months earlier—and I thought we'd moved past it. And it was about *chicken feet*.

Of course, because this played out on social media, the public had plenty to say about me:

> *You're so pushy and rude.*
> *You're a terrible host to force food on a picky eater.*
> *You ruined* RHOD*!*

But others had my back:

> *Let's see you eat one of those dog treats then.*
> *Your post is culturally offensive and you should take it down.*
> *Like what's the secret ingredient that makes these dog treats so much better? Xenophobia??*

There were people on my side, and they weren't afraid to use their voices to defend me and what they believed in.

I noticed that this was happening more and more. Once, before work, I checked my social media and read a comment about how I shouldn't be wearing a bikini. Right after I saw the comment, my pager went off and I went into six hours of surgery. When I came back at the end of the day, my followers had responded for me:

If I looked like that, I'd wear a bikini everywhere I went!
What should she wear to the beach then? A pair of scrubs?
Would that be more "professional"?
Who are you to be telling a grown woman what she should or shouldn't wear?

Another time someone made the usual comment about how annoying my voice was and how they couldn't stand me. One of my followers responded, *Yet here you are, commenting on her post.*

Unless the comments were really bad—like something outright racist or inciting violence—I started to just leave them up instead of deleting them. The way the algorithm works, any comment someone leaves results in increased engagement. As Cardi B says, "I want to thank my haters. They be downloading my stuff so they can hear and talk crap about it—but it benefits me." It always baffles me when people follow someone they dislike and take the time to leave a negative comment on their page. Trust me, there are plenty of people I don't care for, but I'm not spending my time following them or going to their pages to leave negative comments. Think about the type of person who does that. They must have a lot of negativity (or jealousy) in their heart. That and way too much free time.

If you are going to make the move to put yourself out there—on social media, in a leadership position, or in any capacity where you have some influence—be prepared to find that some people out there are not going to like you and will disagree with you. Some will disagree respectfully, and perhaps a healthy dialogue can ensue. Others will be outright nasty and completely uninterested in a healthy dialogue—these are the haters. But, as one of my friends says, HATERS stands for Having Anger Toward Everyone Reaching Success. Just think about it this way—if you didn't have much going on for you, they most certainly would not be talking about you. Be flattered that you are a more interesting topic of conversation than something else.

If you want to avoid criticism, here are three things you should do:

1. Do nothing.
2. Say nothing.
3. Be nothing.

That's right—if you do all three of these things consistently, no one will ever criticize you. Easy, right? Okay, I'm being facetious, but I hope you get my point. As soon as you have a big idea, or you're trying to do something different, or you're just out there being yourself, there will be people who dislike you, disagree with you, and spew their negativity at you.

The negativity is unavoidable, but it's also okay. It's simply unrealistic that 100 percent of the people who come across you will like you or agree with you. No one in the world has 100 percent likability—not even Mother Teresa. Let's say right now that your sphere of influence is one hundred people. Out of those people, ninety like you or are indifferent to you, but then there are ten people who really do not like you and who really want everyone to know that. It's that one girl from high school, your work colleague, or your awful sister-in-law. You know who those people are, and you can generally avoid interacting with them. The problem is that when your sphere of influence increases to one thousand people, nine hundred like you, but now one hundred don't. It seems like so many more people dislike you, but it's actually the exact same percentage. These people might think your idea is stupid, your fashion sense sucks, or you aren't an effective leader. And some of them can be quite loud about it or, worse yet, be nice to your face but then say disparaging things (which somehow always seem to make their way back to you) behind your back.

As humans, it is our natural tendency to pay more attention to the negative than to the positive. Psychologists have a name for this: *negativity bias*. This is likely a result of evolution, as our ancestors who paid more attention to negative things and were more attuned to danger had a survival benefit and got to pass down their genes. This bias accounts for why, if you receive a performance review and your boss has nine nice things to say about you and one thing they want you to work on, you will focus on that one thing. In a larger context, that one thing will overshadow all the good things you've done and the people you've affected for the better. It is important for us to be aware of this tendency, which can cause us to dwell on small, insignificant things and cause us worry. Instead, we should try to reframe those thoughts and turn our focus to the positive.

If you feel like you have something to say, something that you want to share with the world, don't be afraid to express yourself out of fear that someone won't like you. Set the expectation that there will be people who won't like your idea so that you'll be prepared when it happens—which it inevitably will. Once you're able to move past that, you'll see all the people who do like your idea and want to work with you on it. Our natural tendency is to think *What will I lose?*, whereas you want to think *What will I gain?* Because so much can be gained—connecting with others, finding a purpose, or making a difference in the world. But none of those things will happen if you choose to dim your light because you're afraid of what someone else might think or say.

JOY PRESCRIPTION

Use Your Voice for What You Believe In

- *Ignore the haters.* Think of it this way—the fact that you've got haters means you're doing something different. If you went with the status quo, never had an opinion, and never put yourself out there, you wouldn't have any haters. Most of the time, what they're saying has way more to do with *them* than with *you*. Don't ever play small because you're afraid of what a hater might say.
- *Speak up when you need to.* If you feel strongly about something, don't just let it go. Don't bury it deep down, where it will fester. Instead, use your voice to express your point of view and feelings. Who knows, maybe you'll find that other people feel the same way or that you inspired someone else to use their voice.
- *Take a digital detox.* If you feel like social media is getting to be too much for you, take a step back. Taking a break can allow you to recalibrate and remind yourself of whom you should be listening to.

CHAPTER 10

LIGHTENING UP

Posing with Aromasthesia candles

ONE OF THE QUALITIES I ADMIRE MOST IN OTHER PEOPLE IS creativity, probably because I don't consider myself to be a creative person, either by nature or by profession. No one wants a creative anesthesiologist, right? Can you imagine if I tried to be creative in the operating room? "Oh, let's see what this drug does today!" I've always wanted to be creative, but creativity just doesn't come naturally to me. Rote memorization, following the rules, and coloring inside the lines are much more my speed. For most of my life,

I stuck to left-brain activities, afraid to express myself in ways other than what people expected of me.

As a child, I was taught that if you aren't good at something (or if it doesn't earn you money), you shouldn't bother with it. If you can't succeed at something professionally or monetarily, it isn't worth it. Unfortunately, this way of thinking led me to give up plenty of interests that might have brought me joy. I never had hobbies growing up because my parents thought they would interfere with my studying. I didn't paint or draw, and, unlike many Asian kids, I didn't even learn to play a musical instrument. Basically, I had no form of self-expression. But for a few years when I was young, I was allowed to take figure-skating lessons, which became my one and only joy in life.

It started when I was around eight years old. My school was giving out a free Saturday pass to the local skating rink if you completed the reading challenge, which was reading fifteen books in a month (something I did every week). The moment I stepped on the ice, I forgot about the kids in my class who made fun of my lunch and my secondhand clothes, my parents' fights about money, and how I still didn't have my own bedroom. Instead, I was gliding across the ice as if my problems had floated away, and I imagined that I could float away too. It was a feeling of freedom that I'd never experienced before.

After that, I begged my mom to take me back to the skating rink. On Saturday mornings, she would drop me off for the free skate, and for a few dollars, I could stay the entire day. Around noon the rink would get cleared, and the skating students would give a demonstration. I would watch as the girls twirled around on the ice and wonder if I could ever be as effortlessly graceful as they were.

When my mom asked me what I wanted for my next birthday, I said I wanted to take a skating lesson. She agreed, and afterward the coach told her, "Your daughter has a natural talent for skating, especially for someone who's never taken a lesson before. I'm really impressed with her skills. If she can commit to a weekly lesson with me, I think she could reach the level for competition."

I knew we didn't have enough money for lessons, but I begged my mom to find a way. "I'll never ask for anything ever again," I pleaded. "Just give me this one thing."

"Okay," she finally said. "But don't tell Daddy."

Over the next few years, I took one lesson a week and quickly fell in love with skating. Besides the fact that it gave me a sense of grace and artistry, I liked that it was a solo sport—it's just you and your skates. You don't have to rely on other people for your success, and no one else relies on you. If you make a mistake and fall, you're not letting anyone else on the team down. This feeling of self-reliance continues for me today, and it's probably not a coincidence that I chose anesthesiology, which in many ways is also a solo sport.

My coach was right. Soon I was good enough to start entering competitions, which opened a whole other world for me. I saw how if you had enough skill, time, and dedication, you could go far in the sport. By this time, my dad knew about the lessons, and he and my mom constantly fought about them. Figure skating was expensive—there were not only lessons to pay for but entry fees for competitions and the outfits that went with them. I don't think my parents understood the purpose of hobbies. My dad never did anything for fun except fishing, which was utilitarian, as we ate every fish he caught, and all I ever saw my mom do in her free time was take care of the house and our family. Occasionally, after dinner, she'd turn on *Wheel of Fortune* and sew or knit. My mom understood how much I loved skating, and she tried to support me, which often created conflict with my dad. Whenever I didn't place at a competition, I felt a sense of shame and that I was letting my parents down. Here they were, scrounging up every cent so I could skate, and I couldn't even show them that it was worth their sacrifice.

The other girls at the skating rink were a different breed altogether. They had money to spend on new costumes, while my mom and I would buy a plain secondhand one. The night before a competition, my mom would stay up all night painstakingly gluing crystals on it to jazz it up a little for me. The other rink moms were like the skating version of dance moms—they'd hang out at the rink with snacks ready for their daughters after class, whereas my dad would drop me off early in the morning and I wouldn't see either of my parents for hours. I had only one lesson a week, and I put everything into it. Sometimes I would see some of the other girls complaining, crying, or sitting down during their lesson. Not me—I treasured my forty-five minutes and never ever complained to my coach. To save money, I devised a scheme to let my dad know when I was ready to be picked up. I would go to the pay phone at the rink and place a collect call to my house. When the operator asked my mom or dad if they would accept the call, they would say no, but that way my dad knew it was time to come pick me up. Thinking back now, it seems like a silly thing to have done. A quarter was just a drop in the bucket compared to the hundred dollars a month it took for me to keep skating, but we saved where we could.

By the time I was thirteen, it was clear to me that I wasn't headed for the Olympics and that there would be no way to pay my parents back for everything they had sacrificed to pay for my skating lessons. At this point, some of the other girls were getting homeschooled so that they could spend all day practicing at the rink. I was going to school seven hours a day and skating for two, but they were skating for seven hours a day and going to school for two. I knew my parents would never agree to that. Also, deep in my heart, I knew that even if I could take more lessons, I just didn't have the innate talent that some of these girls had. My footwork and spins were good, but I was never a powerhouse for jumps. My best was never going to be good enough. I should cut my losses and focus on my studying.

The day I decided to give up skating for good was after a regional competition. Neither of my parents had attended, but my dad picked me up afterward.

"How did you do?" was the first thing he asked me after I got into the car.

"I...um...placed third," I mumbled.

He didn't even glance at me in the back seat. "I didn't pay two hundred dollars this month for you to enter a competition and place third. Why do you spend all this time and money to skate and you can't even win?"

I felt a wave of humiliation and disappointment wash over me. *My dad was right*, I thought. There was no point in entering competitions, or even in continuing to skate, if I wasn't going to be the best at it. Why spend money on something when I couldn't show a tangible reward or any outward achievement for it?

The next day I hung up my skates. I didn't set foot on the ice again until I was in college, when my boyfriend at the time asked me to spend Christmas break with his family in New York City. He took me to the ice rink at Rockefeller Plaza so that we could skate around the enormous Christmas tree. It was a romantic thought, but stepping on the ice reminded me of all my bittersweet feelings toward skating—something I had once loved but had made me feel like a failure. I told him I wasn't feeling well and wanted to go home.

Skating will probably always be something of a sore spot for me, intertwined with my other complicated feelings about my childhood.

FAST-FORWARD TO MY TIME AT CORNELL UNIVERSITY, WHERE I studied day and night to get into med school. The one fun class I got to take was the Cornell School of Hotel Administration's famous Introduction to Wine class, notorious for being the most failed class at the university. Since I was only nineteen, I wasn't legally allowed to drink and had to apply for a special waiver from the professor who taught the class. I argued in my application that because it was my senior year, it was my only chance to take the class, and if I didn't, I'd be missing out on an esteemed Cornellian experience. The professor signed off on the waiver.

My expectation was that the class would be fun and easy, a reprieve from developmental physiology and biochemistry. Boy, was I wrong—it was definitely not a blow-off class. On campus, you could always tell who was taking the wine class because we had to carry around a little black case padded with foam contain-ing three wineglasses that read "Cornell Wine Expert." I felt so sophisticated walking around campus with that case. In class, the professor passed around a bottle with a stopper in it that allowed us to pour exactly one ounce. Anyone caught trying to get extra was promptly kicked out. When everyone had a pour, the professor instructed us to observe its color. Was it pale yellow like straw or golden like honey? Then, holding the glass properly by the stem, we swirled it to mix some air into the wine and observe its "legs"— the wine left on the inside of the glass after you swirl it. Then we repeated the swirling and took a good whiff.

"Don't be shy about it. Stick your nose right into the glass and take a good three-second inhale," the professor said. "What do you smell? Leather? Tobacco? Ripe berries? A wet rag? There's no wrong answer here. Everyone has their own interpretation."

I appreciated that last part, since in almost every other class, there most certainly was a wrong answer. Finally we got to take a sip of the wine, but not just a normal sip like you'd do with water. No, here we were instructed to hold the wine in our mouth, purse our lips, draw some air across the tongue over the wine, and swish it around slightly, making an audible gurgling sound before swallowing it. The whole process was like a ritual, and I loved it.

I'd tasted wine before but not really *tasted* it. When I was growing up, wine was in an aisle at the grocery store that my parents never went down. My dad would sometimes drink *baiju*, a Chinese grain alcohol that can be up to 120 percent proof and frankly smells like rubbing alcohol. At college parties, it was all about beer pong and taking shots, but wine was something grown-up and worldly.

I had no idea that wine could be so complex. For one thing, it had never occurred to me that it could come from so many different places, like Argentina, South Africa, and Australia. I guess it was just something I'd never given much thought to. Aside from arriving from China when I was six and going to college in New York, I had never traveled outside Texas. Wine had an aura of exoticism and romanticism that made me realize there was more to the world out there.

Learning about wine also appealed to the nerd in me. I pored over the textbook, *Wine for Dummies*, and devoured information about different terroirs, malolactic fermentation, and the *méthode champenoise*, which was used to make champagne for over three hundred years. Winemaking has a rich history intertwined with environmental changes, politics, and technology. The process of growing and producing wine is one-third science, one-third art, and one-third luck. I also loved that it took time to taste wine and that it was a social activity. In my stress-filled life, wine was slowing things down for me. Previously I had spent all my time studying and worrying about getting into medical school, but learning about and tasting wine gave me an immediate pleasure that I very much needed.

I finally got to visit my first vineyard in person when I was doing my residency in San Francisco. Daniel loves wine, and we started going to Napa Valley as a getaway from the city when he came to visit me. I loved learning about the history of all the vineyards—how they got started, how they were passed down through families, and how the owners ran them today—and I asked a lot of questions. At one tasting, I guess the owner thought I knew more about wine than the average visitor (I kept talking to him about phylloxera, a parasite that preys upon vineyards), and he wondered whether Daniel and I were interested in getting into the business. That is how Three Moons Wine was born.

The "three moons" in the name refer to Daniel, his father, and his brother because it started out as a family affair. Basically, Daniel convinced his father and his brother to make the initial investment with him and work with a professional winemaker to make their debut cabernet sauvignon. The resulting two hundred cases—which is a minuscule amount compared to what a typical winery produces—were then served at family-owned properties and family gatherings, and the rest were given away as gifts to friends. The overwhelming response was "Where can we get more of this wine?"

As nice as it was to be able to bring a bottle of Three Moons Wine to a dinner party, what I enjoyed most about making our own wine was the process. Finally, since the days of learning about wine in college, I was able to geek out in real life over details like what percentage of petit verdot we should blend in and how many months we should age the wine in new French oak barrels. Every fall we would go to Napa for the harvesting of the grapes and watch them being picked, sorted, and crushed. There were always lively harvest parties and traditional "wine stomps," done more for fun than out of necessity, as in the olden days. (Thank goodness for that because I really don't need my cabernet tasting like feet.)

Until 2019 I was mostly just an observer in this process. Occasionally I would give Daniel some suggestions on what blends I preferred, but he made the final decisions with the winemaker. He drinks mostly red wine, but I prefer white. To me, a chilled glass of white is the perfect beverage for a hot Saturday afternoon.

One day Daniel suggested, "Why don't you try blending your own white?"

"Do you think I can really do it?" I asked. "What if it sucks?"

"People just like to drink wine…even if it's crappy wine, which this won't be. Plus, if no one likes it, you'll just have more to enjoy yourself."

I liked the idea, but I was still doubtful. What if my wine was a huge flop? Before, there had been no pressure because the wine was attributed to Daniel. With this wine, everyone would know it came from me. What if people said, "So she took one wine class at Cornell fifteen years ago and went on a few tastings, and now she thinks she's a master vintner? Ha!"

When I expressed my misgivings to the winemaker, he said, "You know more about wine than most people. I think it'll be fine. Plus, I'm here to help you. What do you want? An oaky, buttery chardonnay? Or a crisp, fruit-forward sauvignon blanc?"

"I want a white that's not too sweet, definitely not buttery," I said. "More dry, like my sense of humor."

He smiled. "Do you want to keep the name Three Moons for your wine or change it up?"

"Let's just keep it the same."

As I said, creativity was never my strong suit, and there was no better name for a wine that I could think of. I did, however, want the meaning to change. Whereas previously the "three moons" had been Daniel, his brother, and his dad, my wine's three moons would be my twin daughters and me. Over time, the moons had evolved, just as I had. My wine would reflect me, my tastes, and my journey from someone who was scared to try anything she wouldn't be good at to someone who was willing to take a chance in order to express herself.

∼?

FOR MY NEXT NONCREATIVE CREATIVE ACT, I BECAME AN ENTRE-preneur by accident.

During the first few weeks of the pandemic, my anxiety was through the roof. After I put the kids to bed, I found myself pouring a glass of wine, often two, on more nights than not. One day I was on a Zoom call with my therapist, talking about my anxiety.

"It's just hard for me to turn off my brain at night," I said. "The only thing that really helps me is the wine. As soon as I taste it, I know it's time to wind down and let the day go."

"What else could you do?" she asked. "Is there something else you like to do that we could use as a substitute behavior rather than pouring yourself a glass of wine?"

I thought about it as I looked around the room. "Ummm, I really love candles," I replied meekly. "I have certain ones that are relaxing, which I burn when I need to calm myself, and others that are more energizing that I burn when I need to write a paper, clean, or orga-nize my closet."

"Okay, now we're getting somewhere," she said. "Instead of pour-ing a glass of wine, could we associate lighting a candle as the signal to your brain to start winding down?"

Why not both at the same time? I thought but didn't say out loud. My therapist wasn't a huge fan of my jokes during our therapy ses-sions, especially when I used them to deflect from something else.

I firmly believe there are two kinds of people in the world: those who love candles and those who couldn't care less about candles. I happen to fall into the first camp. There is *always* a candle burning at my house. I have different candles that I burn for different moods. Under deadline to finish a book chapter for an anesthesia textbook? I burn something with citrus, which is energizing and uplifting. Had a rough day at work and just need to relax? The go-tos are anything with lavender or eucalyptus. Feeling snazzy and can't wait to put the kids to bed for some mommy-and-daddy time? Anything with amber or vanilla will help me get in the mood. Basically, my husband can come home from work and determine how I'm feeling based on what candle I've got burning.

When I burned certain candles, I noticed that my allergies were worse. I took a deep dive into how candles are made and learned that paraffin wax, which is the prime ingredient in many candles, is made from petroleum as a by-product of producing gasoline and emits volatile organic compounds. There was no "ingredients list" on a candle, so I couldn't be sure what was in the candles I was burning. Since I couldn't control what other people were putting into their candles, I decided I was going to make my own. I went online and bought all the necessary supplies—glass, wax, essential oils, wicks, and pots to melt the wax in. Then I turned the basement, which was Daniel's wine cellar and man cave, into a makeshift candle factory. It gave me a goal-oriented activity that made me focus on something instead of sitting around and worrying.

Because anesthesia was all I really knew, I named the candles I created after anesthesia drugs. The ones with relaxing scents like rose currant and jasmine bamboo I named after the go-to-sleep and relaxing drugs, propofol and Xanax, respectively. The more energizing scents like citrus vanilla and saffron jasmine I named for the time-to-wake-up and resuscitation drugs like sugammadex and epinephrine. I added drug facts on the back with "active ingredients" like tranquility and magic fairy dust. Then I made funny "indications for use," like *If anyone has ever told you that you have a resting bitch face* or *Continued lack of fruition on dating apps.* Finally, I added some potential side effects, such as *When you light this candle, you might feel the sudden urge to take a bubble bath.* The thinking was that I was "prescribing" this candle to whoever was using it. Creating these candles gave me a way to be quirky and humorous in dark times—and, quite frankly, it gave me something to focus on other than work and family.

When I was done with my first batch, I had twenty candles. I couldn't possibly use them all myself, so I decided to send them to some of my health-care friends with a handwritten note:

> Just wanted to say that I'm thinking of you and hoping you and your family are well. I recently started making candles as a stress-reliever and wanted to share one with you. If you can smell this—congratulations—you don't have COVID! Love, Tiffany

Lo and behold, I got a bunch of messages from my friends telling me they loved the candles and asking how they could order some to send to their friends. Before I knew it, my hobby had become a small business. I had my own candle line. I decided to call it Aromasthesia, combining my two passions of aromatherapy and anesthesia.

Once I had come up with six different scents, I took some pictures on my iPhone and started an online store with a preformatted template I purchased for a hundred dollars. I copied the link and sent it to about fifty friends with a little note saying, "If we've all got to be stuck at home, at least you can make yours smell nice! Please consider supporting my new business Aromasthesia!" *Easy,* I thought. But then I started to find out it wasn't so easy.

In the beginning, about 10 percent of my candles broke during shipping because I didn't know how to pack them properly. (Who knew they needed to be double wrapped and put into a box inside another box? Was UPS playing kickball with my packages?) The first month I received over a hundred orders, and my assistant and I were up until 2 a.m. pouring candles in the basement. I once discovered a candle with one of my hairs stuck in it (thank goodness before I shipped it out). And then came the issues with inventory management, the supply chain, and finding a place to manufacture the candles that wasn't my basement. The first two years, I didn't spend any money on advertising, but in year three, I tried to take out some online ads to grow my business. However, they were all taken down because it looked like I was trying to sell Xanax, propofol, and ketamine online. I was like *Oh my gosh, noooo... they're just candles!*

I've had a steep learning curve as an accidental entrepreneur, but turning my candle-making hobby into a business has also given me more than I ever expected. At first it freed me from my anxiety over the pandemic by giving me something else to focus on. Then it allowed me to exercise the creative side of my brain—the side that I hardly ever got to show. I've gotten to stretch other muscles by learning about customer acquisition, online marketing, and quality control—admittedly not the most exciting of topics, but ones that are necessary for my business to grow.

Finally, my candle business gives me the opportunity to connect with others, not just friends but other people whom I would otherwise never have met. For example, when I first started, I had doctors ordering candles to give to their nurses or medical assistants as gifts because they appreciated the medical theme. They wrote to me and told me these were the best candles they'd ever smelled and that the "possible side effects" on the back label made them laugh out loud. I also listen to feedback from customers who don't resonate with the medical focus and are looking for something more mainstream. And ever since I sold my first candle, I donate a portion of my profits to local charities in my community.

Do I wish that I had stuck with figure skating as a child, even as a hobby? I don't know. But I recognize now that in extinguishing the flame of enjoyment for an activity that didn't need to be so competitive and stressful, I lost some of the ability to love doing things just for the sake of doing them. In my mind back then, and for a long time afterward, I felt that I either had to be the best at something or shouldn't do it at all. If I wasn't a success, then I was a failure. This kind of dichotomous thinking really limited what I thought I could do in life.

As an adult, I've decided to embrace my interests for the sake of enjoyment and not accomplishment. I'll never be a champion figure skater. My wine label and candle line will most likely not land me on the Fortune 500 list. But I've learned that it's okay to do something just for the fun of it. And it's never too late to do something that expresses our creativity, allows us to grow, and brings us happiness.

JOY PRESCRIPTION

Explore Your Creative Side

- *Make a list of what you always wanted to learn or get better at.* Think back to when you were a child. What did you enjoy doing? Did you like to draw, but along the way you stopped because someone told you that you could never be an artist or you weren't good enough? What's keeping you from doing those things now? It's never too late to learn something new or do something that lets you grow as a person.

- *Learn along the way.* Oftentimes we won't do something creative because we convince ourselves that we don't know enough about it or that our ignorance will show and we'll be ridiculed. We talk ourselves out of it before we've even had the chance to try it. Don't let your lack of knowledge about something stop you from pursuing it.

- *Share your enthusiasm with others.* With any hobby, there will be others who share your interests. This is also a great opportunity to make new friends. Choose something you enjoy, and I bet that you can find a community of others in real life or online whom you can talk shop with and learn from.

CHAPTER 11

SKIN DEEP

Learning to be unapologetically me

HERE ARE SOME RULES I LIVE BY:

- Whenever you have a problem, drink some water. (This may not solve your problem; I just think everyone needs to drink more water.)
- Aim for seven to eight hours of sleep per night. (If you live by the saying "I'll sleep when I'm dead," your death is probably coming a lot sooner.)

- Always wear sunscreen. (It is much easier to prevent damage than to undo it.)

Yes, all these things have to do with skincare, which is one of the topics that people ask me the most about on social media and in real life. I'll happily spill my skincare secrets to anyone who will listen, because I think taking care of your skin can be a vital and rewarding process. It can be a calming activity, it can make you feel more in touch with yourself, and it can boost your confidence—you don't feel like you have to hide behind layers of makeup because you're already putting your best face forward.

I didn't always feel this way. In fact, it's taken a long time for me to feel comfortable in my own skin. When I was a little girl standing in the checkout line at the grocery store with my mom, I'd look at the models featured on the covers of the fashion and lifestyle mag-azines. They always looked so beautiful, so carefree...and so white. I never saw anyone who looked like me on those covers or on TV. Back when I was a kid, Asian American women just weren't featured that often in the media (and if they were, they played the same ste-reotypical roles). I'm glad that it will be easier for my daughters to appreciate being Asian because there is more Asian representation now than ever before.

When I was growing up, my mom always warned me, "Don't go outside too long or you'll get too dark." She wasn't worried about skin *cancer*—she was talking about my skin *tone*. In many Asian cultures, for many centuries and even today, darker skin is associated with getting a tan from working in the fields while paler skin means that you are well-off enough to stay inside. Nowadays this belief has translated into an all-consuming obsession with keeping yourself from getting a tan (literally, in Chinese, 晒黑—*shài hēi*, or "getting dark"). My parents' friends from church would say, "Tiffany's so cute," and my mom would reply, "Yes, except she's so dark." This can really make a person develop a complex about their skin tone (and is one of the reasons why I always wear sunscreen and a huge hat).

My mom had her own skincare routine that involved whitening and brightening creams, but I always thought she was beautiful just as she was. I remember being around ten years old, sitting on her bed after she had taken a shower, watching her rub the serums and lotions onto her face, which was as smooth and pale as porcelain. When I asked to try some, she'd give me a little bit. I felt like I'd just been handed a magic potion—I would smell it, admire the color and consistency, and rub it onto my cheeks, making sure to cover both of them evenly. Skin care is an interest that we still have in common. In her midsixties now, my mom still performs her nightly ritual, and I often share products with her that I like. Her skin remains light and poreless, and even though there are a few wrinkles now, it is still radiant.

It wasn't until I was a teenager that it occurred to me that my skin tone could be a good thing. At that time, all the popular girls in high school were going to tanning beds.

One day one of them gestured toward me and said, "I want to be as tan as Tiffany." She turned to me and asked, "Where do you go? Do you go to Planet Tan?"

"Ummm, no, I don't tan. This is just my natural skin color," I said.

"No way, lucky! I would die to have your tan skin."

All my life, I had been told by my mom that I was too dark. I'd sneak her whitening cream from her vanity and put it on my face, hoping that it would transform me from an ugly duckling into a swan. But now here was a popular girl saying she wanted to be my color. It was okay—even desirable—to have my skin tone. *Thank goodness I'm in America and not China*, I thought. It was the first time I felt pretty on the outside, even though I still didn't feel pretty on the inside.

For the most part, my parents left me with the impression that cultivating an aesthetic sense and caring how you looked were in direct opposition to becoming an educated, successful person. Beauty and fashion were on one side of the scale, mathematics and science on the other, and it was clear which of these sides took precedence. If my mom ever caught me with a copy of *YM* or *Seventeen* magazine, she'd ask me why I was reading trash and tell me to go find a real book instead. At school, though, I started looking for a different kind of validation—an external one that didn't involve studying or getting good grades.

As clumsy as my early attempts with makeup were, they were a way to express myself and allow me to be a little rebellious in my own way. I would take the money I made babysitting and ride my bike to the grocery store to buy wet n wild lip gloss, mascara, and eyeliner—the last one was easy to hide because I put it in my pencil case. At home, I didn't have much privacy, and my mom once caught me with a lip gloss and threw it in the trash. After that, I wised up and started hiding my makeup in a hole in the back of a teddy bear that had ripped. When I got to school, I'd go straight to the girls' bathroom to apply my makeup. Soon I learned that it was impossible to put eyeliner on my hooded Asian eyelids—it always transferred or smudged. I ended up looking like I had two black eyes. But when I had lip gloss on, I felt more confident and stood a little taller. Ultimately, I think makeup helped boost my confidence and give me a glimpse of what my future could hold.

Then there was the hair-dyeing incident. I was bored with my jet-black hair and decided I wanted to have blond highlights, so I bought a bottle of Sun-In. I sprayed it liberally all over my head, just like the instructions said, and went outside to let the sun do its work. Let me tell you, Sun-In does *not* work on Asian hair. Instead of golden highlights that suggested I hung out at the pool, I gave myself chunky orange streaks that reminded me of my stupidity and vanity every time I looked in the mirror. There was no way to hide it. When I told my mom what had happened, she confirmed that I was stupid and vain. It didn't even occur to me to ask her to take me to a salon to get it fixed. I was grateful that she didn't slap me for what I'd done.

In addition to makeup, I used my money to buy clothes that were the height of fashion for teenage girls in the late 1990s, including baby tees, JNCO jeans, and Airwalk shoes. String thongs were another "must have" item at my high school. The trend was to have the side string coming out from your low-rise baggy jeans so that everyone could see your underwear. The six-dollars-per-pack Hanes underwear that my mom bought me was just not going to cut it. So after school, I went to the mall with a friend and spent my hard-earned money on a pack of string thongs from a store called Gadzooks, along with some baby tees from Wet Seal.

After years of wearing secondhand clothes from garage sales and being made fun of for my cheap, ugly sweaters, I figured out that the secret to being popular wasn't only being blond and tan; it was also wearing clothes from Abercrombie & Fitch. I begged my mom to buy me a thirty-dollar Abercrombie T-shirt, but she refused to pay that much money for a T-shirt with a silly logo on it—and rightfully so. I didn't really care what those clothes looked like; I just wanted to fit in. It's funny how when you're young, all you want to do is fit in, and then once you are older, you just want to stand out.

By the time I got to med school, I had started to develop more of a sense of personal style. I would go to class in a cute outfit and heels—I was even voted "best dressed" my senior year. My friends Lisa and Michelle understood that clothes were a fun way for me to experiment, but I'm sure some of my classmates must have thought I was crazy getting dressed up for a biochemistry lecture. Still, since I was at the top of my class, no one questioned it. I was starting to learn that I could be a good student *and* express myself through something I was interested in.

⟳

YOU KNOW HOW I SAID BEFORE THAT NO ONE WANTS A CREATIVE anesthesiologist? Well, no one wants a fashionable anesthesiologist either. I mean, I rock my scrubs as well as anyone can, but there is a time and place for expressing personal style—and the hospital is just not the place. I've gotten used to people trying to write me off because I'm a small Asian woman—I've frequently been asked, after I've been speaking to the patient for ten minutes and introduced myself as their doctor, when "the doctor" is coming. And I can't tell you how many times patients or their family members have said, "*You're* our doctor? You look too young to be a doctor." So, as you can imagine, I don't really take chances with the way I present myself at the hospital. I take my job very seriously and maintain a straitlaced demeanor because I know my patients and their families are relying on me to help them through a very difficult time.

Once I get home, I feel like I can take off my "professional doctor" hat and put on a different hat and talk about my skincare routine or unbox a purse or a pair of shoes on social media. If I'm feeling extra spiffy, I'll do a dance or a funny skit. But that doesn't affect what I did that day or what I'll do tomorrow in the operating room. It doesn't mean I'm any less dedicated to my job because I care about something other than anesthesia. In fact, I started doing a lot of these things on social media *because* my job was so serious, and I needed some kind of outlet. After ten hours in the operating room, I need things that are pretty and fun to take my mind off the stresses of work. I fully believe that having other interests actually makes me a better doctor.

For a long time, I hid my love for beauty and fashion from my colleagues at the hospital because I didn't want them to think I wasn't serious about my career. I concealed this side of myself so that they wouldn't think my interests detracted from my passion for medicine, research, and teaching. If I did let my guard down, I was often met with confusion, lack of interest, and even disapproval.

One Monday morning, I was chatting with some colleagues in the doctors' lounge about what we'd done over the weekend. A male colleague mentioned that he'd played golf, while another had gone hunting. Then it was my turn.

"I went to Fashion Week in New York," I said, which was the honest answer. "It was fun but really hot. I was running from show to show and sweating all over the place."

No one said anything. Then a man asked, "Who was looking after your kids while you were away?"

"Their father," I replied.

I doubted that he would have asked that if I'd been a man. No one wonders who looks after the kids while a man plays eighteen holes of golf. And these comments don't just come from men; they come from women as well. I think we've all internalized a bit of the double standard that some leisure activities are more appropriate than others, especially when they fall along gender lines.

It seems like if you're a working mom, your hobbies can't be purely for yourself—they have to be something like cooking, gardening, or decorating—something that helps your family or improves your home. But you know what really improves the home? A happy, refreshed parent who's just spent the afternoon doing something they love. Anything that makes you a more well-adjusted person will make you better at work and at home because you'll be happier.

I recently went to an anesthesiology conference where the speaker presented data on a survey question that was asked of both male and female anesthesiologists: "Have you ever felt that your clinical ability has been doubted or taken less seriously because of your gender?" Out of the men who responded, only 7 percent said yes, compared to 87 percent of the women. I was disheartened to hear this but not shocked. Any woman who works in a male-dominated field knows what it's like to have to maintain a certain demeanor so that you're taken more seriously. In the operating room, if a man orders people around, he's strong and assertive. If a woman does the same thing, she's considered strident and bossy (and possibly another word that begins with *b*).

I became even more aware of this double standard when I became a working mom. Once, when my girls were infants, I was in a faculty meeting during which they announced that they were putting together a new hospital committee and asked who might be interested; I raised my hand. Several weeks later, a friend asked why I wasn't going to the meeting for the new committee that afternoon, which confused me. I found the committee chair and asked him why I had been left off; he said in a paternalistic way, "I thought it probably wouldn't be a good idea to put you on the committee because you have young kids at home." He acted like he was doing me a favor, but I hadn't been consulted, even though the opportunity was something I wanted and would have been good at. But I said and did nothing at the time.

A couple of years later, when I started posting on social media about the challenges of being a professional woman with diverse interests, I got a huge response from women of all ages and from all careers. Many people have told me that they're inspired by the fact that I'm a doctor who also loves things like fashion and beauty. I'll never forget one particular follower who reached out to me. She was a young Asian female medical student with a passion for art. She asked me if she could send me a drawing, and I agreed. Not long after that, I received in the mail a picture in which I'm depicted on one side in my scrubs in an operating room and on the other side in an evening gown. In the bottom corner, she wrote "#SheCanBeBoth." This was something I wished I had known growing up—that it's not either/or but *and*.

After receiving this drawing, I started using the hashtags #SheCanBeBoth and #SheCanDoBoth on social media to honor all the different dimensions of myself and other women out there—because we *can* be both. I found that other women were using this hashtag as well to celebrate the fact that we can thrive in multiple roles and careers. And that we won't be boxed in.

As they say, beauty is only skin deep. You can be skilled at using makeup or do everything right to take care of your skin but still feel ugly. We work so hard all the time to be pretty on the outside, but we don't pay enough attention to what's going on inside. It has taken me years of work to finally feel at ease in my own skin, to be able to admit to and be proud of my interests in beauty and fashion, and to embrace all the different sides of myself. I know now that we can be good at what we do—and maybe even better—if we take the time to have fun, pursue other interests, and be ourselves. The only person who's really stopping us from accomplishing our dreams is the person who's looking back at us in the mirror.

JOY PRESCRIPTION

Be Your Authentic Self

- *Consider whether you are overly concerned with what other people think of you.* Are you a people pleaser? How does your preoccupation with what others think of you affect your relationships, your daily actions, and your decision-making? Ask yourself, at the end of the day, does it *really* matter what other people think? (Most of the time, the answer will be a resounding no.)

- *Don't let people weaponize professionalism against you.* What you choose to do when you're not at work is your business. As long as it's not illegal or hurting anyone, your time outside work should be spent as you see fit. If this ever happens to you (as it did to me), consider saying, "Please explain to me how this has any impact on the quality of the work I perform." The judgments that others make about your extracurricular activities are just that—judgments. Teachers, doctors, pilots—frankly, everyone—deserve to be themselves without the fear of being called unprofessional for simply living their lives.

- *Think about the long-term benefits of fully showing up as yourself.* What's the best thing that could happen if you showed up as your true self? Stop hiding parts of yourself that you're worried others may not like or understand. How much could showing up more authentically benefit you and your relationships? Would you feel more confident and self-assured in all aspects of your life and therefore function at a higher level, whether at work or at home? Most of the time, you will find that you have much more to gain than to lose.

CHAPTER 12

IF YOU DON'T LAUGH, YOU'LL CRY

Performing stand-up comedy at
the Laugh Factory in Hollywood

T'S A COLD WINTER NIGHT AT THE DALLAS COMEDY CLUB. I'M standing backstage as people are starting to come in. The club holds about a hundred people, and I'm poking my head through the curtains to see how it's filling up. I've invited my brother, Josh, my friend D'Andra, and a few doctor friends. I have *not* asked my parents.

Tonight I'm going to be onstage performing stand-up comedy for the first time.

Breathe, I tell myself. *You can do this.* I've spent the past two weeks practicing my routine forward and backward. I've been on other stages plenty of times—usually at medical conferences, talking about novel techniques and drugs in anesthesiology or presenting research findings from my clinical trials. But those talks were guided by PowerPoint presentations, and there was certainly no laughter expected from the audience. This is completely different. They say the most common fear in the world is glossophobia, or fear of public speaking. Well, here I need to speak publicly *and* make the audience laugh. Let's just say I am scared shitless.

I've had exactly two drinks. Previously I'd been testing the ideal number of drinks to give me the optimum blood alcohol concentration to loosen up a bit but not get sloppy onstage. I figured out that one was not enough, because I was still jittery and nervous, and three drinks was too many, because I started messing up my material.

So with two vodka sodas in my system, I strike a few power poses and prepare to do my first (and maybe last) stand-up comedy routine.

"Please welcome Tiffany Moon!" the emcee says.

It's showtime.

❧

YOU MIGHT BE WONDERING WHAT BUSINESS I HAD DOING A stand-up comedy routine. Never in my life had anyone used the word *funny* to describe me. Most of the time, I felt that people were laughing *at* me and not really *with* me. Sure, I had been unintentionally or sarcastically funny at times, but never purposefully funny.

Since I started learning English when I emigrated from China at age six, I didn't know what was considered funny in America. We didn't have a TV in the house until I was eight. And even then, all we had was a thirteen-inch black-and-white box we got at a garage sale that had terrible reception. We wrapped the rabbit-ear antenna with aluminum foil to try to get a better signal. Still, watching TV shows like *Full House* and *Saved by the Bell* helped me learn English, since we always had closed captions on. And the laugh track accompanying these shows taught me what was considered funny. That laugh track was pretty much the only laughter in my childhood.

Slowly I started to understand American humor. Kids on TV were always either getting into trouble with their parents (something I didn't dare do) or ending up in ridiculous situations with their friends (of which I had none). In real life, the kids around me at school played pranks on one another and made fun of the teacher; I was the smart girl whom my classmates would try to cheat off, but I was never in on the jokes. I longed to be a part of their pranks and experience laughter like the other kids.

It wasn't until I left home to go to the early college entrance program that I felt like maybe my childhood was funnier than I had realized at the time. Once, I confessed to my roommate Vanessa that my mom used to throw a *tuǒ xié*—a slipper—at my head whenever I did something wrong. Whether it was getting a 92 percent on a test, placing third in a spelling bee, or talking back to her, my head was the target, and her weapon of choice was her house slipper.

"I have a weird question…did your mom ever do that to you?" I asked Vanessa.

"Of course!" she replied. "We call it *la chancla*."

Literally, *la chancla* is a flip-flop, but it didn't matter. Both my Chinese mom and Vanessa's Spanish mom appeared to favor throwing footwear at their kids' heads as a form of discipline. And it wasn't just shoes. Vanessa and I bonded over the fact that at some point, our moms had thrown a wooden spoon, the remote control, and a stapler at us. We laughed for a long time over this.

Even though we had grown up in different cultures, we had this in common, and our shared childhood experience brought us even closer together.

Another shared experience that we bonded over was our moms making us lie about our age if it meant saving money. Growing up, I remember a Chinese restaurant that we went to on special occasions. With the purchase of two adult buffets, kids under six years old were allowed to eat for free. For years when we went there, my mom would remind me that I was five years old, even though I was really six...seven...eight years old.

One day the manager went up to my mom and said, "Excuse me, ma'am, but I believe your daughter has been five years old for three years now."

"No, my daughter, she only five years old," my mom argued.

I got my meal for free that day, but the next time we went back there, I was allowed to be eight years old, and my mom paid the kids' buffet price.

Later, when I started getting on social media, I did a series of Tik-Toks about my mom. I wore a wig that resembled my mom's sensible bob and spoke in an exaggerated accent. Most people got that I was making fun of my mom out of affection and were able to relate to it in some way. Ever had something thrown at you because you got a bad grade? *Check*. Ever wore jackets inside during the winter because your mom wanted to save on the electricity bill? *Check*. Ever asked your mom why she couldn't just pack you a ham-and-cheese sandwich for lunch like everyone else? *Check, check, and check*. Poking fun at the way I had grown up not only made me feel better about my childhood but also connected me with other people who'd had similar experiences.

Through social media, I became friends with a few comedians, including one who was doing a comedy show in Dallas. She asked me to emcee the show, and I agreed. Then, about two weeks before the show, she called me.

"It looks like one of our comedians had to drop out. Can you take her place?"

"Ummm, I don't think that's a good idea. Emceeing is one thing, but I don't think I can do a whole stand-up routine. I'm really not that funny...."

"No, you're so funny. I've seen your TikToks," she assured me. "It's only ten minutes. Just get up onstage, be yourself, tell some jokes, and everyone will laugh. Can't wait to see you, okay, gotta go, bye!"

And that's how I landed my first stand-up gig at the Dallas Comedy Club. I think that if I hadn't done *RHOD* and put myself out there on social media, I wouldn't have had the guts to do this. As with *RHOD*, I thought this was an opportunity for personal growth and something I probably wasn't going to get a chance to do again. I would rise to the occasion. I'd watched plenty of comedians before, and they made one-hour shows look easy. Surely I could do a measly ten-minute set, right? All I had to do was go up there and tell a few jokes, and then I would have enough experience to add "stand-up comedian" to my CV.

Soon I found that stand-up comedy looks easy only because the people who do it are professionals. Like athletes, they have been honing their craft for multiple hours a day for the past several years. This was not something I could pull off in two weeks, no matter how hard I tried. Even if I'd had four weeks to come up with something, I don't think it would have made much of a difference.

When I sat down and started to write my routine, I realized I had made a terrible mistake by agreeing to this. I started to imagine bombing my set and embarrassing myself. Then I started thinking of what all the haters would say—*What the hell, now she thinks she's a comedian? She sure wasn't funny on* Real Housewives. In a state of panic, I called my friend.

"I'm sorry, I don't think I can do this. I'm worried I'm going to bomb. I don't need to give the haters more ammunition to make fun of me. Can you find someone else?"

"Eff the haters," she said. "You see any of those idiots putting themselves out there?"

"But what if I do really bad?"

"And what if you do really good?" She paused. "Plus, we already sent out the email with the lineup, so you're doing this."

Well, shit. Again I approached this challenge the only way I knew how—I went on Amazon, typed in "How to do stand-up comedy," and bought the first book that popped up, *How to Kill in Comedy* (ironic, since I normally helped save people, not kill them). Then I grabbed my notebook and went on Netflix to watch some comedy specials starring comics I loved like Jo Koy, Ali Wong, Kevin Hart, Anjelah Johnson, Ronny Chieng, Tiffany Haddish, and Gabriel Iglesias. I took note of how each comedian had their own flavor of comedy and certain mannerisms that were unique to them. Sometimes it was what they said that was funny, or an exaggerated pause or facial expression, or the way they moved their body. I felt like each of these comics whose performances I studied were having a conversation with the audience or telling a story about their life. The situation didn't have to be inherently funny—sometimes the situation was mundane, and then something unexpected happened that made it funny.

I tried to think of my comedy routine as a collection of stories from different parts of my life, from growing up in an immigrant household to being supersheltered and not knowing anything about sex or drugs to all the weird things that I saw during medical school and residency. The problem was that I had all these random stories, but it was hard to make them fit together and flow well. I wanted to tell a story about how my mom prides herself on never buying any napkins or ketchup—when I was growing up, we had a drawer full of napkins from all the fast-food places we frequented and another drawer full of ketchup and sauce packets. To this day, I don't think my mother has ever bought a bottle of ketchup. *Why buy what you can get for free?* was my mom's motto. But how was I going to transition from that to a story about the bizarre things that people have told me when they wake up from anesthesia, like the guy who told me he'd killed someone or another man who asked me in the recovery room to marry him? It wasn't that I had a scarcity of funny moments from my life—I just didn't know how to put them all together. In comedy—as it is frequently in life—it's the timing, the delivery, and the transitions that make all the difference.

Most comedians, when they're starting out, test their material on friends who are in the business or go to open-mic nights to practice. I mostly just practiced my material on my husband. Although we have a similar sense of humor and usually find the same things funny, it's different when you're trying out jokes on your spouse. First, I had to scratch all my marriage jokes, like the one about how in every successful marriage, one person is crazy and the other person is boring. (I didn't think he'd appreciate me referring to him as boring.)

Poor Daniel had to listen to me tell joke after joke. One of them started out like this: "There are only two people in the world who care when you last ate—your mother and your anesthesiologist...."

"Why does your anesthesiologist care?" he asked.

"How can you not know this?" I exclaimed. "We have to know so that if you have a full stomach, we can take precautions so that you don't aspirate!"

"What's 'aspirate'?"

"It's when your stomach's contents go into your lungs, which can make you very sick or even die. Duh! How do you not know this? How can you be married to me and not know this?"

Exasperated, I stormed out of the bedroom. The stress of preparing to do this stand-up routine was getting to me, and I cursed myself for agreeing to do it. But I knew there was no going back.

The turning point for me was when I decided to stop approaching stand-up so methodically and to just let go and have fun with it. I realized that I really had nothing riding on this, and that thought was freeing because almost nothing else in my life was like that. When I stopped treating it like something I *had* to do versus something I *got* to do, my perception shifted. Whether I bombed or did well, it wouldn't really matter in the grand scheme of things, so I might as well try to have a good time.

Even though it didn't matter, I still wanted to do a good job, so I reached out to another friend who had done stand-up comedy before for advice. Since he lived in LA, we had a Zoom session for me to practice. I ran through my set with him, and he gave me some pointers.

"I'm planning to talk about how my stepdaughter convinced me to do a TikTok dance challenge to the song 'WAP' by Cardi B," I told him.

"You know what?" he said. "Instead of just *describing* it, you should just *do* the WAP dance onstage."

"Seriously? I can't dance! What if no one laughs? What if I'm just rolling around on the floor out there, making a fool of myself?"

"Trust me, they'll laugh."

So that was what I did. I got down on that stage in the Dallas Comedy Club and did the WAP dance, and everyone thought it was hilarious. For those of you wondering, "WAP" does not stand for "web application protocol" or "wings and pizza." It involves gyrating your hips and rolling around on the floor to lyrics that include "Now get a bucket and a mop." My friend was right—sometimes a little physical comedy can go a long way. It was a bit of a gimmick, and I'm not sure I would do it again, but it loosened up both me and the audience.

You might ask, why did I decide to do the WAP dance? When you're doing stand-up comedy, you have the creative liberty to be crass, use foul language, or explore topics that may be a bit taboo. At work, I felt the need to be prim and proper, but onstage, I could be a more naughty, out-there version of myself—which was still me. I wasn't adopting a different persona; I was just showing another side of myself that I had previously hidden away out of fear that people would think I was unprofessional. It felt good to let this other side of myself out into the open, and it felt good to make other people laugh.

The feeling that comes from performing comedy in front of a live audience is exhilarating, satisfying, and terrifying all at the same time. It's a shot of adrenaline like no other. I don't really remember many other details about my set—it was like I had blacked out (and not from drinking). After the show I was completely wiped out (partially from having practiced the WAP dance so many times before I went onstage), but I felt a sense of accomplishment. This time, it had nothing to do with getting a good grade, earning an award, or making money. I put myself out there in front of a live audience, made people laugh, and, most importantly, had fun while doing it.

A month after my show at the Dallas Comedy Club, my comedian friend asked me to do another show that she was putting on for charity at the Laugh Factory in Hollywood. I hesitated at first, but I will do just about anything for a good cause, so I said yes. Now, you might know the Laugh Factory because pretty much every comedian who has made it big has performed there. I did not think I deserved to stand on the same stage as Robin Williams, Jerry Seinfeld, and Dave Chappelle. But instead of letting my fear win, I thought about this as another opportunity to have fun. Also, I wanted to improve on the jokes that hadn't gone so well the last time. After all, I was still me, which meant I wanted to do a good job. However, this time, doing a good job didn't mean that I did everything perfectly but that the audience and I were having fun together.

Doing stand-up is kind of like having sex—the first time, it's scary and awkward and you're not sure what to expect, but the second time, you at least know what to expect. This time, I knew I wanted to be more myself. At the Dallas show, because I was going to do the WAP dance, I had to wear pants and sneakers. For LA, I wore a pink dress and stilettos—not what the typical female comedian wears but what I feel the most comfortable in.

My friend had recorded my first set on her phone, so I had her send it to me so that I could watch it and rework the jokes that didn't land that well. If I thought watching myself on *RHOD* was painful and cringey, this was ten times worse. Nevertheless, I took note of which jokes landed well and which didn't and reworked my routine, adding some new material.

I leaned in to the doctor jokes because after all, you do what you know. I talked about how every few months, someone comes into the emergency room in the middle of the night, needing general anesthesia for a foreign object removal. The story is always the same—they slipped and fell on something. That something has included a flashlight, a Barbie (headfirst, in case you're wondering), a billiard ball (the green 6, again, in case you're wondering), and a screwdriver.

The excuses are also always the same:

"Doc, I'm not sure how it happened...."
"My girlfriend put it there...."

"I was getting out of the shower and slipped. . . . "
And what, the flashlight was just there in the bathroom, stand-
ing straight up, covered in lube?

I had a great time doing that set at the Laugh Factory. I got to meet a lot of other comedians who remain my friends to this day, and we raised a sizable sum for charity. The experience reinforced for me that stand-up comedy is not my calling and that I should keep my day job. But it's still something I'm glad I did because I learned so much about myself in the process, and I have a newfound appreciation for those who make other people laugh for a living.

In fact, I think everyone should have to give a ten-minute stand-up comedy routine in front of a live audience at least once in their life. Why? First, a huge amount of self-reflection and personal growth goes into writing your material and reworking it until it's in good enough shape to be performed. Then there's the performance itself. Ten minutes is a long time to be onstage with just a microphone and no fancy lights, backup dancers, or anything that distracts the audience from you. You have to rely completely on yourself and the connection you make with the audience.

Finally, you get immediate feedback from the audience. If a joke doesn't land, instead of perseverating on what went wrong, you have to keep on going. It doesn't mean the rest of your jokes won't work, but if you get derailed and let it get to you, you jeopardize the rest of your routine. To take an analogy from my childhood, it's like performing a figure-skating routine—if you don't land your combination jump and fall on the ice, you don't have time to react. You have to get back up, find your place in the music, and continue until the very end. You can't let one mistake ruin the whole rest of your routine. Later, you can go back and analyze what happened and decide what needs to be improved, but for the time being, the show must go on. For me, that was a lesson that applied not just to figure skating and stand-up comedy but to life.

⌒

DOING STAND-UP COMEDY MADE ME REALIZE SOMETHING ELSE about my life. For a long time, laughter was not something I consciously sought out. It wasn't there when I was growing up, and as an anesthesiologist specializing in trauma and cancer surgery, my day-to-day was anything but funny. As a person who was anxious about work, my family, and life in general, I needed to add the laugh track to my life, but I didn't know how. I used to look for it externally by watching funny shows or waiting for other people to make me laugh, but doing stand-up made me look for the humor within. To my surprise, when I got down to it, I found that you can find humor in almost every aspect of life. Humor can make you put something in perspective, and then you'll realize it's not all that serious.

I've always thought that if you can't find the humor in a situation, you're missing a little bit of what it means to be human. That was the old me—always stoic and straight-faced in order to display my seriousness, aptitude, and professionalism. But that simply wasn't allowing me to show all the different sides of myself, and it wasn't making me happy. Being able to laugh is what allows us to deal with the difficulties that are part of everyday life. If you can make fun of yourself, then other people will laugh *with* you and not *at* you. If you acknowledge that you have a particular shortcoming, others can't make fun of you for it because you've already beaten them to the punch. Many comedians use self-deprecating humor—Kevin Hart makes jokes about being short, Gabriel Iglesias refers to himself as "fluffy," and Ali Wong calls herself a pervert. I told my audience from the outset, "I just want to remind you all that my day job is putting people to sleep, so know that if you're getting drowsy during my set, it's just because I'm really good at my job."

Laughing with others, I've found, is a great way to feel less alone. A long time ago, I laughed with my roommate over the random stuff that our moms threw at us. Years later, many more people at a comedy club laughed with me as I told them what it was like growing up in a strict immigrant household. "Unlike most Asian parents, my parents didn't put a lot of pressure on me growing up. They said I could go to any medical school I wanted to." Being able to laugh over shared experiences is what brings people together. In a world that's divided over just about everything—from religion to politics to cultural identity—to be in a room full of people laughing at the same joke feels unifying. For one small moment in time, you forget your differences and celebrate the fact that sometimes we're more alike than we are different.

Everyone is going through their own problems. But what brings us together, what creates connection, is being able to laugh at ourselves together. I've always believed that if you don't laugh, you'll cry. So why not laugh? Laughter is truly the best medicine and should be a part of any prescription to finding joy in life.

JOY PRESCRIPTION

Find the Funny in Life

- *Write a comedy skit.* Even if it never gets performed in front of anyone, think of a humorous story from your life and write it down. How would you tell it to make it funny (almost any situation can be funny if you tell it right)? Even if you never perform it, you'll have an interesting and funny story in your back pocket to pull out at cocktail parties.
- *Get up and dance.* Whether it's by yourself or with others, attempting the latest TikTok dance challenge or just finding your own groove, physical movement can be freeing. It's impossible to be in a bad mood while twerking—try it, I dare you.
- *Try to find the humor in a situation.* It's all about mindset. For example, someone cut me off the other day when I was driving, so I slammed on the brakes. My kids lurched forward in the back seat: "Mommy, what happened?" Instead of being angry or annoyed, I told them that the driver in front of us had massive diarrhea and needed to go home and change his pants. My kids and I laughed hysterically all the way home. Situation: still the same. Mindset: too blessed to be stressed.

CONCLUSION

JOY IS A FUNNY WORD. WHEN I WAS GROWING UP, I DON'T think I knew what it meant. My only familiarity with it was from the song "Joy to the World," which I learned in church. My parents never spoke of joy or happiness. I think what happens when you're an immigrant and you grow up with scarcity is that you believe that you can't afford joy. You end up focusing on other things that you *think* will bring you joy, like achievement and success.

I used to think that joy was a destination. *If I just get into medical school, then I'll have joy. If I just get married, then I'll have joy. If I just have children, then I'll have joy.* And don't get me wrong— each of these events brought me immense joy, but my anxiety often prevented me from being wholly present and enjoying the journey; instead, I was singularly focused on the destination and what was next. I grew up being told that working hard and achieving things would make me happy. My entire self-worth was wrapped up in achievement. I was checking off the items on my to-do list of life, but I still wasn't feeling fulfilled because I was too busy to enjoy the process or consider whether my approach was actually right for me. In fact, most of the time, I felt overworked, underappreciated, and confused. But I kept going and achieving, often to the detriment of my own mental and physical health, because it was all I knew. If I didn't continue to work hard and achieve, who would I be? If I wasn't useful to my family, friends, or patients, how would I demonstrate my worth? I was running around frantically trying to save everyone else when the person I needed to save most was myself. Once I saved myself, then I could be wholly present for others in a joyful, meaningful way.

I won't pretend that I have it all figured out. There are days when I'm frantically running around and feel that nagging pinch of anxiety. I still have to remind myself not to try to fit more into my day and just be present, that it's okay to just *be* and not *do*. But I'm no longer looking for perfection, just progress. I'll probably always be a work in progress on my journey to discover and embrace the things that bring me joy in life. The difference is that I'm better equipped now to do it in a way that is true to my values, allows me to grow as a person, and strengthens my relationships with others.

These days, I no longer look at achievement as the measure of my worth. Yes, I've accomplished many of the things I've set out to, but I've also learned a few things—many of them the hard way. I've come to realize that true freedom and fulfillment come only when we live life on our own terms. That we need to seek not only opportunities to cultivate self-knowledge and self-understanding but also love and connection. That we have to question the roles and expectations others have imposed upon us and say no to those roles if they're not working for us. That we can find joy in the in-between moments and the journey rather than just focusing on the finish line. And it always helps if we can remember to laugh a little along the way.

ACKNOWLEDGMENTS

THIS BOOK WOULD NOT HAVE BEEN POSSIBLE WITHOUT THE guidance, love, and support of so many people. To my 姥姥, 姥爷—thank you for taking care of me when I was little. I hope you're looking down from heaven and are proud of me. To my parents—thank you for inspiring me to work hard and never give up. From you, I learned the values of determination, resilience, and dedication. To my husband, Daniel—thank you for letting me be who I am and loving me unconditionally. You are the yin to my yang and definitely my better half. I would not be where I am today without you. You have supported me through climbing the ladder in academic medicine, filming for a reality TV show, and becoming an entrepreneur and author. Thanks for putting up with me making you film TikToks and reels. To Nathan and Nicole—it's been incredible watching you grow into a young man and woman—I am so excited to see what the next stage of your life is. To my family—thank you for your encouragement and understanding when I locked myself in the study for hours at a time to write. Josh—I'm so glad you turned out okay even though you never had to save some gum to chew later or eat half-rotten fruit. All joking aside, I'm incredibly proud of you and all that you continue to do. Mindy and Milo—even though you can't read—thanks for keeping me company and for licking the tears off my face when I was writing the sad parts.

Wendy—you were instrumental in making this project come to life. Thank you for helping me get the thoughts from my brain into the words on the paper. I'm glad we had that week in the summer together, and I'm sorry you had to watch *Real Housewives of Dallas* season 5. Jessica—thank you for your editorial direction and making sure I said what I meant to say. Roger—I can't believe we first started this conversation over three years ago. Thank you for being by my side every step of the way—you believed in me from the very beginning, and your encouragement and support have meant so much throughout this journey. To my team at Hachette—Dan, Nzinga, Connie, Sean, and Amina—thank you for shepherding me as a first-time author through this process. It has been so rewarding, and I'm grateful to have such an amazing team. Jonny, Tamie, and Tang—thanks for making me look good and feel good. I can't believe we've been working together for almost ten years now.

To my sister from another mister, Vanessa, thank you for being a sister to me and teaching me to twerk in our dorm room at 1 a.m. You were the first one who taught me to be brave, take chances, and have fun. To Lisa and Michelle—we will always be the Happy Triad. I'm so glad that we didn't get kicked out of medical school after that penis prank. We have literally learned to become doctors, gotten married, and had children while supporting one another, and you girls mean the world to me. I'm grateful that we still prioritize our friendship and make time for a Triad Trip each year. Adam—hey girl, hey! You made living in SF so much fun; thank you for being my gusband. There's no one else I'd rather be getting yelled at with for being too silly. You always make me laugh, and I love you dearly. Thank you to my friends who continually support and uplift me— Sunny, Bonnie, Vicki, Peter, Karen, Amy, Judith, Crystal, Nicole, Guerdy, Mora, Betsy, Tracy, Ssonia, Jessica, Eboni, Joyce, Maddie, Tama, Dina, Kathleen, Kelsi, Tama, Micah, Lea, Kellie, and Ted.

To my readers, followers, and fans—thank you for letting me shine without being afraid to dim my light. I sincerely hope that I have brought a smile to your face and more joy to your heart. Thank you for the love, support, and advice you've given me through the years.

To my daughters, Chloe and Maddie—being your mom is my greatest joy. Always remember that Mommy loves you.